"*Living on the Other Side of Fear* is a remarkable book. It is a story of the healing journey of an incredible woman. And her story is amazing. I read it in one sitting, unable to put it aside. It continues to haunt me. Above all, it continues to heal me.

The book is filled with wisdom, an ethereal wisdom that goes far beyond conventional self-help books. You will sit there dazzled as you read. And you will know that Ms. Villaverde has tapped into something so profound that it is life-changing. Yet, as profound as it is, it is accessible, washed in practicality and in the deepest of beliefs in the possible.

I urge you to open yourself to the power of this book because in doing so, you, too, may get to live on the other side of fear."

Sidney B. Simon, Ph.D.
Professor Emeritus, Psychological
Education, the University of Massachusetts

"If *The Celestine Prophecy* touched your spirituality and *The Bridges of Madison County* your emotions, you must read Hilda Villaverde's new book, *Living on the Other Side of Fear*. It is an incredible combination of both, which will leave you with amazing insight and joyous tears of wonder and delight."

Sherry Henry
Pres., Interwestern Management Co.
& General Manager, Fiesta Inn

"The opening sentence in *Living on the Other Side of Fear* is 'I was born afraid.' As frightening as this may sound, from the beginning of her life, the little girl of Indian and Hispanic descent from a small town in Arizona learned to meet difficulty with intelligence, sensitivity, and determination. With gall and gifts she found her way to prosperity. With tenacity and trepidation she found her way to successful relationships. If you are looking for inspiration and quantum lifestyle changes, read her book and you will clamor for more."

Mary Alice Edgerton, D.D.
Founder, Seminary Services Network &
"Bookies" for first-time authors

"In *Living on the Other Side of Fear*, Hilda Villaverde presents a personal account of a life transformed from fear into love. Hilda challenges the reader to confront and befriend fear, using its gifts and messages to live a life ever more fully rooted in love. Readers will find both comfort and challenge in these pages. As in life, they will be challenged to look into themselves and ask, 'Do I choose love or fear?' And, as in life, they will have the opportunity to embrace the comforting message: 'You are not alone....'"

David Jecmen, Ph. D., Psychologist

Living on the Other Side of Fear

A Spiritual Passion for Life

Hilda Villaverde

Published by:
PLUMA PUBLISHING INC.
10105 E. Via Linda # 103-296
Scottsdale, AZ 85258
800-584-1989
FAX: 480-657-9355
E-mail: hildapluma@aol.com

ISBN 09669607-0-X

First Printing, 1999

Cover, interior illustrations & design: Penelope Greenwell
Back cover photograph: Dan Coogan
Editing: Jayn Stewart

Printed in America

If you are unable to find or order this book from your local bookseller, you may order directly from the publisher.

Heartfelt Thanks

To All My Relations

Deep gratitude and love to my son, Ron, who chose to come and join me this time around. To my husband, Joe Schneider, for the love, safety, and support which he created in our home, where this writing was birthed, I will be forever grateful.

Thanks to my dear friends who have supported me and encouraged my writing: Karen Piper, Joani Cihak-Solvesky, Susie Mitchell, Patty Crawford, Kimberly Chavez, Susan Marchese, Diane Cowdrey, Philis Kendler, Marie Ravenscroft, Lisa Koschka, Lilly Burchinal, Rev. Linda King, Tammy Reading, Sally Cooper, and Dina O'Brien.

My heart is filled with gratitude for my editor, Jayn Stewart, my midwife. I love you for your unconditional love and talents. To Bob Day, my business partner and spiritual coach, thank you for believing in me, for listening, and for not allowing me to give up. I cherish our friendship and hold you in my prayers always.

I also thank those who have supported Vision Gatherings, Inc.: Vickie Stripp, for her patience and caring, Jim Peak, David Jecmen, Michele Kaplan, Dan Gates, Lee Robert, Cherie Veatch,

Nancy Sommer, Ed Price, and my dear Veronica Escalante. Because of you, others will be blessed.

And finally, my gratitude to those who came into my life to assist me in my physical, emotional, and spiritual healing: Dr. Leon Asadourian; Dr. John Reed; Drs. Frank and Marilyn Powers; Arlene Tolen, M.P.H.; Linda Frazee; Elaine Willis, Ph.D.; Dr. Marilyn Wells; and my special spirit-filled friend, Dr. Kathleen Hosner. You have given me the gift of true joy and filled me with passion for life.

Dedication

This book is dedicated to the mothers I have had in my life:

For my mother Maria Ramirez, who gave birth to my physical self and taught me how to love deeply in my most painful relationships.

For my mother Dee Toci, who taught me how to make love to myself and gave me the gift of true friendship.

For my mother Maggie, my sister, whose love challenged us both, forced us to go beyond the limitations of family love, and brought us the gift of sisterhood.

For my mother La Rae Whitehead, who insisted I develop a relationship with books and words and encouraged me to go beyond my small-town beliefs.

For my mother Sherry Henry, who graced my life with adventure and unconditional love for all people.

For my mother Mary Alice Edgerton, D.D., who enlightened me and cultivated my spiritual growth.

I dedicate these words to them with honor and respect for their womanhood.

Hilda

Table of Contents

Introduction...1

One..............My First Encounter With Death.............5

Two..............A Mystical Experience............................11

Three..........School Years.......................................21

Four..............Breaking the Bonds...............................33

Five..............On My Own.......................................43

Six...............My Son Ron......................................61

Seven...........Birthing My Spirituality.......................71

Eight............A Turning Point..................................83

Nine..............My Spiritual Journey...........................97

Ten................Teaching, My Life Purpose.................107

Eleven..........Luz...117

Twelve..........My Ministry.......................................129

Thirteen........Give Us This Day Our Daily Bread....141

Fourteen........And God Created Hairdressers........147

Fifteen...........The Search For My Roots..................155

Sixteen..........Fear, the Beloved Adversary.............163

Affirmations..171

About the Author...173

Introduction

𝓘 was born afraid. Inside my mother's warm and safe womb, I was overwhelmed with knowing that I would soon enter an unknown, frightening space. My birthday, May 30, 1950, coincided with Memorial Day, the holiday which commemorates those who have lost their lives in fighting and conflict. Somehow, even before my birth, I knew that I would mourn the loss of my childhood and that I would live in constant conflict with fear. Becoming free from my fears would become the struggle and commitment of my life.

The book you are about to read is a story of the only two emotions that exist — fear and love — and of my journey from fear to love. Fear, as I have experienced it, is the root cause of anxiety, anger, denial, depression, and despair. Love, as I experience it, expresses itself in hope, vitality, purpose, courage, compassion, passion, acceptance, and connectedness to all life. This is the story of how I survived and even grew to use the benefits of fear. It is also a book for millions of other people who have experienced terror and lost trust in themselves and others.

When fear becomes a dark presence looming over us, we begin to doubt our own identity and self-worth. We see the world as a hostile place and life as a battleground. We move from battle to battle, from one crisis to the next. For many, including myself, this is normal. This — I thought — was life.

The journey of such a life often begins with the abuse of a child. Children are open and vulnerable, and their spirit can be shaped in so many ways. My story is one of physical, verbal, emotional, and mental abuse. My experiences were similar to those of children in many families whose members suffer silently and secretly. Eventually, the secrets become internalized as fears which prevent a healthy connection with the outside world or with a higher power — that which we call God.

How do we handle these overwhelming childhood experiences? Many deal with terror and doubt by succumbing to apathy and darkness or by acting out in negative ways. Others search for love and acceptance by living in service to other people, even at the expense of themselves. Still others overachieve, trying to prove their worth to themselves and the rest of the world. I understand these ways of coping and have experienced them all.

The message of this book is not just about surviving, but about learning to live an outstanding life of joy, peace, and love. It is the story of how my pain and fear led me to courage, determination, and spiritual unfoldment. In my journey of abuse and terror, a near-death experience as a child, encountering an earth-bound ghost and angelic beings, and meeting my own guardian angel, Emma, I have discovered that fear itself is not the challenge. The challenge lies in uncovering our fearful self and coming to terms with it. Once we bring to light our fears and the thoughts that create and empower them, they begin to disappear.

Ultimately, this is a story about the search for truth and the discovery of the power of the mind, the strength of the heart, and the gifts within each moment of existence. When I began to creatively *respond* to my fears instead of *being* my fears, I opened to a higher dimension of being. I could feel my connection to God and the Universe. The fear I came to know and love is the story of my good news.

At the end of the chapters I have included what I call "Little Bolts of Light," which are followed by short affirmations. These "bolts" are my insights related to the chapters. I invite you to take a moment to reflect on your own meaning and interpretation of these thoughts.

One

My First Encounter with Death

At the age of six, I died. This I recall completely. I had gone into the hospital for a routine tonsillectomy and come home after three days. I remember feeling tired after the surgery, and yet I could not wait to play with my two sisters, Connie and Maggie, and our older brother, Carlos.

We lived in the small town of Ajo, in southern Arizona. Our family is of Mexican and Indian heritage. Our dad worked as a laborer in the copper mines during the day and as a drummer at night in a band that played in local bars. Mom stayed home to raise her four children. Our home consisted of three rooms and a tiny bathroom off the bedroom, which we four children shared with our parents.

Just home from the hospital after my tonsillectomy, I sat at the window watching Mom leave for the grocery store. Her last words resonated in my mind: "Do not go outside to play! You need to rest!" As soon as I could no longer see her, I made a mad dash for the outdoors.

5

A neighbor had brought a new toy over to play with. It was something called a "hula hoop," a magical, lightweight hoop one could move around the waist, hips, legs or throat. I wanted to feel it around my throat. We took turns with the hoop, laughing and clapping our hands to encourage the next one to rotate it faster and keep it going longer. My turn came several times. Each time I was able to sustain the rotation longer and faster around my waist. Finally I placed it around my throat, proudly sustaining its rotation for quite some time.

And then it happened. From deep in my stomach I felt an upward surge of movement. I opened my mouth, and huge globs of blood poured out. Old coagulated blood and fresh blood flooded my mouth. I couldn't stop coughing. I choked and gagged, unable to catch my breath. My head began to feel light and I began to spin. I could see the panic in my playmates' faces. I felt myself fading away.

I don't remember how we got to the hospital, but my next memory is of lying on my mother's lap in the waiting room. A bucket sat next to us on the floor to catch the blood that trickled from my mouth. My mother wiped my forehead with a wash cloth as we waited for the doctor to see us. My entire body ached. I faded in and out of consciousness.

I recall waking up in bed in a hospital room. Mom

was at my right. She held my hand, and her rosary
— her string of beads used for constant prayer —
was wrapped around my hand. She looked numb,
staring at the priest on my left. He had placed a
white linen cloth with a cross on top across my
chest. I.V. tubes were connected to my frail arms,
and another tube protruded from my mouth. A
man with jet-black hair was crying painfully at the
foot of my bed. It was my father. He cried loudly
and uncontrollably, holding my feet and stroking
my legs. He called my name over and over, begging
me not to leave. I found myself hovering above the
scene:

> *I am looking down on what is happening. I
> feel safe, warm, light, secure, healthy and
> whole. I love this feeling. I have no fear. I am
> aware that someone is with me. I do not know
> who it is and I do not need to know. This is the
> most perfect place I have ever been.*

> *In his native Spanish my father cries, "Please,
> God, do not take her from us! Please God, let
> her stay!" I am moved by his love for me,
> which I have never experienced before. He
> makes promises that touch my heart. "If you
> let her live, I will never drink again. I will
> change my ways and treat my family better. I
> will never put a hand on my child again. God
> forgive me for the things I have done to my
> family. I don't want this to happen to me!"*

I cannot believe what I am hearing. I want so much to believe his promises. My entire young life I have lived in terror. We all live in terror of this man we call our father. He drinks and loses control often. He beats our mother and our sister Maggie regularly. The rest of us are also abused, physically and verbally. Each morning we awake in fear. I dread each day. What will it bring? What will happen to set off my father? I cannot remember a single moment of joy. Many times I have wanted to die. It is the only way I know to get away from this childhood in hell.

Here I am, hovering above my body, watching my parents — my father the violent abuser, my mother the ultimate victim. I cannot believe there is a God, or if there is, how He can allow this to happen. "God, you have forsaken me...."

I do not hear the voice, but I sense it: "Look down and see what is happening. Do you want to stay with them, or would you like to leave now? It is your choice."

I hear my father's cries and promises. "Please God, let her live! I will change my life for the better!"

Caught up in the intensity of the moment, I

respond, *"I want to stay. I want to see our family together. I want to live in a family that is safe for all of us. I do not want to leave my mother, mi mama. I want to be with her and protect her. What if I leave and something happens to her? I have to stay! I can't leave now!"*

The next morning I awoke. I was back in my body in my hospital bed. I was very cold and in pain, but I felt safe. I could not wait to go home — to my new home, to my father who loved me. I was so excited to experience not being afraid that I began to fantasize a new and different life for our little family.

I stayed in the hospital for several weeks. During that time I received blood transfusions. My blood type is unusual, but the hospital found an older man, an Anglo, who kindly donated his blood for me. He also came to visit me after the transfusions to see how I was coming along. I enjoyed being in the hospital. It was safe and I felt loved. Mom visited every day, but Dad never came again.

Finally, my mother brought me home. I couldn't wait to see my sisters and brother, and especially Dad! I waited all day for him to come home from work. As he walked in the kitchen door, I ran to him and threw my little arms around his waist. He tightened his body and peeled me away. Looking down at me, he said, "Get away from me. You are no longer my daughter. You don't have my blood. You are not my child any more."

I will never forget those words or what I felt as long as I live. He had made a promise to God and a promise to me, and he had lied. I was devastated. I was engulfed in fear once more. It didn't take long for the drinking, yelling, and beatings to begin all over again.

Little Bolts of Light

My passion for life began at the young age of six. Clearly I chose to live. And at that tender age I affirmed my role as caretaker for my mother. How beautifully this has blessed me in my relationships with women. Years later my therapist would profess the healing attributes of women connecting with women: "Every relationship you have with another woman is filtered and expressed at the same level of commitment and love you have had with your own mother." My love for women was established then. I died so that I could develop my life purpose of service and empowering other women.

Affirmation:
I choose to live.

Two

A Mystical Experience

$\mathcal{I}$t was summer, a year after my near-death experience. I dreaded being home all day with nothing to do. We children were allowed only a limited time to play with neighborhood friends. Dad did not like to have other children in our home. It was too disruptive for him, and he did not want to be involved in any activities that he could not control. Most of our summer days were spent anticipating when he would leave for work and dreading the moment when he would come home. My most important thought was buying time before the next violent incident.

Sometimes we took short holidays. They were nightmares. Dad played "games" with us. At the time, I thought they were scary. Now I know they were inappropriate, dangerous, and abusive. His favorite game was pretending that he was losing control of the car, especially on steep mountain roads. It was terrifying to feel the car traveling at high speeds and jerking back and forth. We were tossed all over the back seat. Our mother pleaded with him to stop, but that only encouraged him to become even wilder in this "game" with all our lives. Mom's pleas and our frightened yells seemed to please him. I dreaded another summer when I would have to spend even more time with this man.

Our summer trip that year was to the Grand Canyon. This led to an event that brought me to my second experience with death, but under entirely different circumstances. It showed me the subtle interplay of worlds: the life we know on earth, and the life we have yet to experience — the life after death.

Our plans were to leave early in the morning for the seven-hour trip from Ajo to the canyon. The night before, Mom was still sewing, no doubt finishing some last-minute stitches on our new play clothes. We never had store-bought clothes. She made all our clothing from flour sacks and other inexpensive fabrics. I remember fondly the taste of the tortillas that she made with the flour and anticipating the new outfit she would make from the sack with her loving hands.

It was late in the evening. Mother sat hunched over the sewing machine. We three girls were lying on the floor next to her, lulled by the sound of her foot on the treadle, which moved back and forth in a relaxed rhythm. Dad was asleep and so was our brother Carlos. Suddenly, Maggie jumped up and screamed in pain, tearing her hair as if to pull something from her scalp. She was in horrible agony, trying to tear away whatever was caught in her thick, black, hair. A large centipede dropped to the floor and scurried away. Maggie's pain was intense. Dad appeared from the bedroom, upset that his rest was disturbed. Maggie was rushed to the hospital but was told that nothing could be done. She would have to endure the pain and fever, which would eventually go away.

In spite of this incident, we left the next morning for the Grand Canyon. I don't remember how long Maggie's fever lasted, but I was worried for her and Mom. Our lives revolved around our dad's changing moods, and we tried to keep things as pleasant as possible.

There is a religious custom in the Mexican Catholic culture called a *manda*. Loosely translated, it means a promise made to God or to his representatives — Mary, or any of the saints — for a healing. As mother prayed for Maggie, she made a *manda* to do something to express her gratitude and appreciation for her healing. She chose San Pedro, a saint whose statue is housed in a small church in the tiny town of Tubutama in Sonora, Mexico. Her promise to God was to make a pilgrimage to the church and to offer money and prayers of gratitude for the healing. Maggie survived the trip, as did we all, but we had to endure more terrifying experiences with Dad behind the wheel.

Several months later we made the trip to Mexico to complete the *manda*. It was a joy traveling with only the girls, something that didn't happen very often. Mom drove Maggie, who was nine, Connie who was five, and myself, age seven. We arrived in Tubutama early in the afternoon. We children knew nothing about the family we were going to stay with. Mom had told us only that they were our cousins, that they were very poor and dear people, and that we must be on our best behavior. We would not mention the fact that there were no beds, running water, electricity, indoor bathrooms, or other conveniences.

Tubutama is a tiny town, nestled in a greenbelt which is nourished by a river. The homes are constructed of traditional adobe: blocks made of a sun-dried mixture of clay and straw, reinforced by ocotillo branches. We pulled up to one of these houses, the home of Anita and David. Anita came out to greet us with open arms and warm kisses, the traditional welcome of our extended family. David was out of town for a few days. The one-room house had hard dirt floors, which were maintained by frequent watering. In the room were a wood stove, a table and chairs, and a small sofa.

To the right of the front door — the only door opening into the house — was a small, narrow room that had been added on. This room was for Anita's father-in-law, who was paralyzed from the neck down. He could only move his head from side to side. He lay in a narrow bed set high off the ground so that he could be better attended to. Our mother told us to approach him and gently kiss him on the cheek, a gesture of love and appreciation for allowing us to stay in their home. I shall never forget how, as I leaned over and kissed him, a tear rolled from his eye. I was a little afraid but didn't dare say anything. To this day I remember the taste of his tear on my lips.

Anita saw that he was crying and said that these were tears of joy. Her father-in-law loved having company and appreciated visitors from the States. She shared with us that in his healthier days he had been quite active. He missed his mobility. But most of all he missed his beloved wife, who had passed away two years earlier.

Mom and Anita prepared a delicious dinner that night. Today I do not know how people can function so well without a refrigerator or microwave or any counter space. Anita and David's lives were uncomplicated and happy. Mom and her cousin chatted about the family and caught up on news concerning friends and other family members. My sisters and I hung around outside and stayed out of the adults' way, the proper thing to do for children our age.

We had brought our own bedding to sleep on the dirt floor. It would be fun to sleep with Mom, to be close to her. The only light in the room was a kerosene lamp. It is amazing how dark it gets in towns without electricity. The only light comes from the moon. The moon was full that night. I remember Mom commenting that it was a bright evening. She told us if we needed to relieve ourselves before going to bed, we had to go together. The outhouse was beyond the back yard, and she would go with us. We declined and decided to wait until the sun came up in the morning. Tomorrow we would complete our *manda* with San Pedro. We would all go to the church to offer our tithes and prayers in gratitude. The *manda* would bring closure to the dramatic event of Maggie's illness.

Life has a way of softening us and giving us moments where we can rest and have periods of joy. This evening was one of those times. I remember giggling and having fun with my sisters, lying on the floor all bundled up just before we fell asleep. It was good to be away from home.

I did not know what time it was when I felt my sister Connie nudging me to wake up. "I have to go to the bathroom," she whispered. Remembering that the floors were dirt, I suggested, "Go over in the corner. Don't go outside. It is too dark." She countered, "No, I am going outside. I will be right back." She crawled out quietly, opening the front door just wide enough to get through. I tried to stay awake until she returned, knowing there were coyotes and other creatures that roamed the desert during the night. She seemed to be gone a long time, and finally I crawled over to Mom to wake her and let her know that Connie hadn't returned. Mom immediately jumped up from a deep sleep, lit the kerosene lamp, and started toward the door.

At that moment Connie walked in. I was so relieved! "Where have you been?" Mom asked. "I was outside, talking to our cousin Anita," Connie answered. Just then, Anita came out from the little room where she slept on a cot next to her father-in-law. She could not have gotten out of the house from that room. The only door in or out of the house was in the room where we slept.

We were puzzled and asked Connie to tell us about the lady she had talked to. She described a woman with long dark hair, which had some gray in it. She was brushing her hair with a beautiful brush, telling Connie that the brush was a gift from her dear husband. She was dressed in a long white gown and appeared to be very sweet. She asked Connie why we were here and how long we would be staying. Connie did not feel uncomfortable answering her questions, although she found it strange that this woman, who she thought was Anita, would ask her something that she and Mom had already talked about during the day.

Mom and Anita listened spellbound as Connie described the lady, their conversation, her dress, and the hairbrush again and again. Anita told us that the woman Connie described was Delfina, Anita's mother-in-law, who had been dead for over two years. This was the woman her father-in-law yearned for and said that he talked to every day. He often told Anita and David of their conversations, saying that Delfina was still with him and would never leave him. Connie had described the dress she had been buried in. But the most important piece of information was the hairbrush. It was a gift from her husband. They had placed it in her hands and buried it with her. There was no way that Connie could have known any of this. It was a night none of us would ever forget.

The next day we went to the church and Mom fulfilled her *manda*. We did not stay in Tubutama and visit afterwards, as we had originally planned. Mom decided it would be best to drive directly home.

Little Bolts of Light

Mystical experiences are not always as vivid as this. Sometimes subtle experiences occur in our lives that we cannot accept until years later, but this does not diminish the gifts they bring. How long do we live without trusting our own inner wisdom and experience? Years later I discussed this event with my sister. Yes, it had happened. The question "why?" had only one answer: It just did. From this event in my early life, my passion for the invisible world blossomed.

Affirmation:

I accept
what I cannot understand.

Three

School Years

My parents were both raised in Mexico and spoke only Spanish, and in "Mexican Town" where we lived in Ajo, Spanish was the only language I heard. Our town of about six thousand people was segregated into three distinct areas. The majority of homes was provided by the company that owned the copper mine, which was the main employer in Ajo. The Anglos, who were the engineers and managers, lived in the hills and had the nicer houses. The Mexicans, who were the laborers, lived down the hillside and closer to the smelter and tailings area of the mine. The Native Americans lived on the other side of town, up against the open pit. Theirs was the poorest section of town.

My siblings and I attended Catholic school with the sisters of the Immaculate Conception. About seventy percent of us who attended the Catholic school were of Mexican heritage, about twenty-five percent were Anglo, and the remaining five percent were Native Americans. We had a very difficult time in school because the sisters spoke only English. The sisters paddled us and verbally abused us and told us never to speak our native language. We were to forget that we were anything but "Americans." In the name of God they were going to beat English and some sense into us.

I remember vividly standing in line one Saturday evening in church, waiting to make our weekly confession. How much could a child of eleven sin? What could possibly be so sinful about us that we had to go through this ordeal every week? My sisters and I were waiting our turn. A girl friend about our age was confessing her sins to the priest. Suddenly the priest came out of the cubicle and opened the narrow door of the confessional where she was kneeling. He grabbed her by the throat, pulled her out, and slapped her across the face twice. "Five Our Fathers and ten Hail Marys!" he yelled. Then he disappeared back inside his cubicle. Our friend walked to the front of the church, sobbing pitifully, to kneel and do her penance. We decided we would never tell the priest anything that would anger him enough to mete out such punishment. Not only were we abused at home by our dad and at school by the nuns, but now even the priests were hitting us.

The kids from the public school hated the ones in parochial school, and, as often happens when one culture doesn't understand the other, fear turned into anger. My sister Maggie and I were called names. Rocks were thrown at us as we walked to school. The humiliation and embarrassment of being Mexican in Ajo was painful to all of us.

Within "Mexican Town" we lived a life rich with many fiestas. Every wedding, baptism, and birthday was a cause for celebration. But life in general was hard, and within our homes many of our parents escaped into alcohol. I suspect that most of the kids I grew up with were disciplined through physical abuse. I could hear yells coming from neighboring homes, and I occasionally saw bruises on the arms and legs of my fellow students. Our dad hit us with a belt or a whip made from a tree limb. Maggie was beaten most often. The excuse was that she was the oldest and should have "known better." Dad did all the spanking. Mom just threatened us. Our nerves were on edge all the time.

The terror at home continued through my high school years. Days in the classroom are a blur in my memory. My mind was constantly filled with the thought of having to go home to an unending battlefield. I have memories of Maggie and Carlos pulling our mother away from Father's violent fists, of running away from the house and jumping into a car driven by our fourteen-year-old brother, and speeding away to a parking lot or a neighbor's home for safety.

I was always tired. Just staying awake during classes took great effort. The energy that went into surviving at home drained me and left me unable to focus on my classwork. Somehow, though, my brother and sisters and I all made it through school. Although we did not fail, we just made average grades. There is no doubt in my mind that if our home had been a safer, more peaceful place, we would have had a more positive experience in learning. I often wonder when I see children going to school what life is like for them. What happens in their homes? I pray that they have it better than we did.

Despite my father's disapproval, I became a cheerleader in my sophomore year of high school. This was the most rewarding and enjoyable experience I had during my school years. I could escape from home and feel the approval of others. I could hide behind jumps and smiles and cheers. I could pretend I was happy.

In order to pay for the cheerleading uniforms, shoes, and other necessary items, I worked weekends at a local motel, cleaning toilets and making beds. I loved it! I could be away from home and I could help with my expenses. I was appreciated and validated. The lady who owned the motel loved me. I was a hard worker, and she never failed to praise my performance.

My father insisted that I ask his permission to attend every game and cheerleading event but waited until the last minute to decide if I could go or not. This behavior worried my mother and me. Mom would have to intervene if he complained that I was gone from home too often. She would present my case: the team needed me, and I was part of a group that I was committed to. He always argued that he had not made the commitment, and that he would have the final word. In this way he tortured me emotionally, not giving his permission until the last moment before I had to leave the house. He would always say yes, but the emotional turmoil that Mom and I had to live through each time was like a horror movie, with one scary scene after another.

My brother had always been our chaperone. He had to accompany his three sisters everywhere. We were not allowed to go anywhere in the evening without him, and dating was out of the question. This put a great responsibility on Carlos. I remember feeling like a young chick being gathered up by the mother hen, tucked under her wings for protection. Only our mother hen was our brother, Carlos.

Somehow, though, we managed to date, and we even had boyfriends. Carlos knew the boys and constantly reminded us of the horrible consequences we would face if we didn't show up at the designated place to return home. We dated in this unnatural and frightening way, always looking to see if Dad was out to catch us or make an embarrassing scene in public. He was capable of these things. Everyone in our neighborhood knew our dad. They had all seen him drunk in the streets, stumbling home. Our neighbors had heard the frightened screams that came from our house.

The pressure that this responsibility put on Carlos at such a young age continues to manifest in challenging ways for him as an adult. He has great expectations for himself and an exaggerated sense of responsibility and caretaking toward the women in his life. At fifty, he has gone through his third divorce. No doubt he lost his childhood, as we all did, to terror, restraints, and demands that left deep fears and emotional scars.

I had one boyfriend, Jimmy. He was the only boy I dated in high school. Jimmy was a star athlete. He was captain of the football team, a great basketball player, and a first-rate hitter in baseball. He was also voted homecoming king. Since I was a cheerleader and pom-pom girl, we had the opportunity to see each other often. We dated when we could, and he asked me to the Junior-Senior Prom.

Jimmy's father was an engineer at the copper mine where my dad worked as a laborer. Both his parents were educated, quiet people. Jimmy was Anglo, what we called "white" in those days, as opposed to Mexicans or Native Americans. He was tall, blond, blue-eyed and very popular. The prom was an important event for both of us, and I really wanted to go. I knew that Jimmy had to come to our house and ask Dad's permission for me to attend the prom with him.

I was nervous for a month. Jimmy and I had decided that we didn't want to sneak around anymore, and I thought this would be a good time for him to meet my father. I longed for a date without a chaperone. I also prayed for a life without fear and deception. I asked Mom for her blessing, and I am sure that she immediately began to pray that Dad would not make a scene.

Jimmy was to come to the house early in the evening, before Dad's favorite TV programs started. We did not want to interrupt his TV time. My father stands five-foot-four inches tall, and Jimmy was just under six feet. I remember asking him not to stand too tall, so as not to make Dad feel uncomfortable. The things I remember sometimes amaze me!

I had prepared Dad earlier in the evening that someone named Jimmy would be coming over to meet him, and I promised that he wouldn't stay long. Jimmy was at the front door right on time. I escorted him in and introduced him to Dad. He did not get up from his favorite TV chair, nor did he shake Jimmy's extended hand. He motioned for him to sit on the couch next to him.

"What do you want?" he asked abruptly, without looking at him.

"I would like your permission to take Hilda to the prom, which is coming up in a couple of weeks, sir."

My father turned and glared at him. "Aren't you Hank's son?"

"Yes sir, I am," Jimmy answered.

My father suddenly jumped up, pointed to the door and yelled, "Get the hell out of my house! I never want to see you here or anywhere near my daughter again!"

I felt as if the house was tumbling down around me. First the ceiling, then the roof, and then the walls were caving in and crushing me. I couldn't breathe. Jimmy quietly walked out the front door while my father screamed obscenities. I started to run toward the bathroom in the back of the house. I wanted to vomit. I wanted to die. I couldn't believe what had just happened.

How could this nightmare continue? Why was this happening to me, to us, to this family? Where was God? My mind was filled with thoughts of death, of killing myself. When would this ugly dream be over?

As I ran through my parents' bedroom to the bathroom, I tripped on the corner of the bed. I fell and hit my head so hard on a chest of drawers that I passed out. What a relief to go away, to feel nothing, even for just a few moments. When I came to, my father was standing right over me. I couldn't move. I could only look up at him. He asked me if I was all right. I couldn't answer him. I couldn't even cry. I couldn't think past this moment in time.

At sixteen years of age, the pressure of living such a tormented life was unbearable. I fervently wished I could die. I couldn't fathom facing Jimmy the next day. How could I take another day with my father? How could all this happen? What kind of God permitted such things?

The next day at school I saw Jimmy and could not stop apologizing for my dad's behavior. Over and over again he assured me that it was fine. "It happened, O.K?" was all he would say. But for me it would never be O.K. I would wonder as deeply as I could possibly think and feel what it would be like not to have the issues that I had as a Mexican. What would it be like to be white and fit into life?

Jimmy and I actually did go to the prom, along with my sister Maggie and her date. Dad must have been working the graveyard shift that evening. I truly don't remember. But I do remember that we never attempted to ask his permission for anything again. Instead, we continued to sneak around and lie. Life seemed to work better that way.

From my birth until I was eighteen, I wanted to die many times. I sincerely believed this was my only way out. And if it wasn't me, couldn't it be my father who would die and leave us alone? The guilt that came along with these thoughts was suffocating. I don't remember a day of breathing freely or a day when death or fear were not foremost on my mind. Afraid to live, less afraid to die. I had been there before as a child. It felt safer to die.

Little Bolts of Light

Fear is about not understanding what would happen if, instead of judging, we chose to understand, or at least not judge. A single thought can move us from fear to acceptance. When I accept myself, I accept others. I begin to understand.

Affirmation:

**I like all of me, and
I know I am always growing into
who I think I am.**

Four

Breaking the Bonds

*T*wo days after my high school graduation, I left home. I moved from my small hometown in rural Arizona to the big capital city of Phoenix. My sister Maggie and two other friends came with me. We signed a one-year lease for an apartment. The rent was reasonable, and I knew that I would somehow be able to afford it myself, even if Maggie and our friends left. They actually did last only a few short weeks, but there was no going back for me.

The apartment was the nicest place I had ever lived in. It was in a small complex of about twenty one-story apartments. The units shared a center courtyard with grass, trees, and flowers. The managers were a lovely older couple, and most of the tenants were also senior citizens, with the exception of the young people in the apartment next to mine. As frightening as it was to be alone at age eighteen in a strange new world, it felt safer than what I had left behind. I embraced my move to Phoenix as if it were my only hope for survival.

I needed to attend a school that would allow me to earn an income as quickly as possible. I had no money for higher education or even junior college, nor did my grades reflect that I might be capable of attending such a school. During high school I had cut and styled hair for a few neighbor women and some school friends. I knew I had a knack for hairdressing, so I decided to enroll in cosmetology school. Cosmetology training six days a week for nine months was exactly what I needed. I walked to school, which was only a few blocks away from my apartment.

To make some money, I took a night job in a department store several miles away from where I lived. Hitchhiking became my mode of transportation to and from work. For months I stood on the streets and trusted that the person offering me a ride would be safe. I never expected any harm to come to me, and it didn't.

As I reflect on those days, I am amazed at my power of determination. I was indeed determined never to return to the home I had left behind. Hitchhiking was, to me, safer than going home, where I was treated with abuse and disrespect. Having to watch my mother, who refused to leave Dad, even while she was being tormented, was not an option for me. Those thoughts kept my conviction strong that somewhere life would be better. And for now, my somewhere was here and now. Hitchhiking was just a temporary phase.

I worked as many hours as I could at the department store and progressed very quickly in beauty school. I soon was able to move on to what they called "floor work," where I could work on clients and keep the tips. I befriended many clients and offered to cook for them on Sundays. In exchange, I ate with them and received leftovers. Sometimes the food lasted me for days. I was grateful to have watched Mom cook her great Mexican meals for us. Now I was able to provide this service to others, which sustained me during this time of being hungry for food, attention, and love. With my three jobs, I felt that all these needs were taken care of.

Many people were kind to me. One woman in particular became my hair client in beauty school. Her name was Polly Gallardo. She was tall, educated, confident — and Mexican. I had never met anyone like her. She held a high position with the state of Arizona. She traveled extensively throughout the country and was respected in the community. She was my first ray of hope. This could someday be me! This beautiful, warm, caring woman began to remove the shell of shame and isolation I had built around myself.

For awhile my apartment became the place where anyone coming from our hometown could crash for a day or two, sometimes longer. Two months before my lease was up, my best childhood friend, Lucia, came to live with me. She was a beautiful Mexican girl, tall and slender, with huge brown eyes. She had beautiful full lips and gorgeous olive skin. We had been friends since the age of eight. We shared many of our most intimate hopes and desires and had much in common. Lucia's mother was an abusive alcoholic. I had often stood outside her house, listening to Lucia's screams and watching as her mother beat her with her fists and pushed her to the floor, kicking her over and over again. Once I looked through the bedroom window and saw a dramatic beating. I wished in that moment to take the beating for her. I wanted so much to take her pain away. We shared so much as friends, yet I do not remember our ever talking about the abuse from our parents. We only shared our dreams and wishes for the future.

I loved having Lucia for my roommate. Unfortunately, she attracted abusive men. One Saturday evening after having been in school all day, I came home, changed clothes, and hitched a ride to my night job at the mall. I was exhausted when I returned after ten o'clock. On the kitchen table was a note from Lucia, letting me know that she was out with someone and would be home late. I was glad to be home alone. My next-door neighbors were having a party and their music shook the walls of my apartment, but I was too tired to worry about falling asleep.

My neighbors were three young men, just released from military service. They had spent time in Vietnam and were celebrating their freedom. Glad to be alive, they partied that evening. It sounded like a full house. One of them had invited me the day before to join the party, and I had said I would see how I felt after a day of school and a night of work. Now, nothing could move me from my comfortable space.

I had just changed into my pajamas when Jimmy, one of my partying neighbors, knocked at the back door, asking if I would like to come over. I thanked him and lied that I wasn't feeling well and would be going to bed. A few minutes later the front doorbell rang, and I thought with exasperation that it was Jimmy again, playing around. I was determined to stay home and get some rest. I opened the door. To my surprise, it was my room-mate Lucia's ex-boyfriend, Gary. She had broken off with him recently, saying he was on drugs all the time. She couldn't cope with his drug habit and his abusiveness. Here he was at my door, stoned out of his mind. I knew the look.

"Where's Lucia?" he demanded.

"I don't know," I answered truthfully.

"Who is she with?"

"I don't know that either, only that she's out. Gary, please go away. I'm alone and need to sleep tonight. Why don't you join the party with the guys next door? You know everyone there. You'll have a good time." I suspected he had supplied them with drugs — this he did for a living.

As I moved to close the door, he blocked it with his foot.

"Since you're the only one here tonight, you'll do."

He pushed the door open, walked in, and locked the door behind him. I stood there, stunned. Everything went into slow motion. He grabbed me by the hair, pulled me to him and repeated, "Yes, you'll do just fine for tonight."

That year a popular rock group, Iron Butterfly, had hit it big with a song, "Ina-gada-da-vida," which lasted seventeen minutes. At the moment Gary grabbed me, this song came on at the party. The sound vibrated the walls and ceiling of my apartment.

I screamed. Gary dragged me by the hair into the kitchen and pulled out a knife from a drawer. He cut the skin on my arms and shoulders with the knife. He dragged me around the apartment into the bathroom where he threatened to drown me in the toilet if I didn't stop screaming and resisting. I hurt physically, but not as much as emotionally. What was happening to me again? Was I destined to be beaten again and again? How could this be happening to me? I thought of the time I stood by and watched Lucia being beaten by her mother, wishing it could have been me. Was my wish being fulfilled? Was I taking this beating for her?

Gary was just like my father, a small man filled with rage and a great desire to hurt others. His violence brought all of my abusive childhood back to mind. I was not going to let this happen again. I fought him and hit him, pulling away with all my might. I could feel him rip a chunk out of my hair. I ran to the bedroom and tried to close the door, but he was right behind me.

I banged on the wall and cried out for my neighbors, but the music was still playing loudly. Could they hear me? Gary ripped off my pajama top as I desperately pounded on the wall. The music stopped; the seventeen minutes were up. Gary threw me down on the bed and pounced on top of me. The back door opened with a crash. My neighbors came running into the room and pulled this violent man off me. I cried uncontrollably.

Yes, they all knew him; he had indeed supplied the drugs for their evening. My neighbors insisted that everything would be fine. "Don't say anything, Hilda, you'll be just fine. Gary just lost it. We're sure it won't happen again. Just forget it." Everyone left and I lay in bed. The loud party continued. Gary had been taken home, and I was going to forget this ever happened.

The next day I hurt all over, and yet I was numb. I'm sure I was in shock. My neighbors did not want me to go to a hospital. They knew questions would be asked, and they didn't want to take the chance of the police getting involved. I kept silent and just cried to myself.

Later that day Gary's father called me on the phone and asked to speak to me at their home. He had found out what happened when Gary returned home covered with blood. His father had questioned my neighbors and knew I had been beaten. Gary came from a very wealthy family; his father was a scientist and had a high-profile position in the community. My three neighbors took me to his home the next evening.

We sat in their living room as Gary's father asked me questions about the incident. Gary sat silently next to him, never looking at me. After hearing my story, his father stood up and in front of everyone accused me of provoking his son into his actions. He yelled and screamed at me and called me horrible names. He threatened that if I ever reported the story I would not live to see the outcome. I left the house, beaten once again. I moved from the apartment a few weeks later and tried to forget the nightmare which had happened during that seventeen minutes. I never saw Gary again.

Today, thirty years later, I have forgiven all of them, but I can never forget what happened. As for my dear friend Lucia, three years after this incident she committed suicide. She left behind a two-year-old daughter to be raised by a drug-addicted father.

Little Bolts of Light

We have all heard the remark, "Be careful what you ask for, you might just get it." As innocent as my request as a child was, to take a beating for my best friend, I created this situation, this gift, for myself. Do we get everything we ask for? Are all prayers answered? Where our attention goes, there it grows? These statements, conscious or unconscious, are affirmations, especially if we hold them tightly in our minds and give them life. How powerful our spoken words are. How powerful our minds are. How different my life would have been if from that day forward I had known the power I held in myself.

Affirmation:
What I give my thoughts to, I create more of.

Five

On My Own

9 graduated from beauty school in record time, just a couple of days less than nine months. My first job after school was with a very busy hairdresser. I helped his pregnant assistant, who would soon be leaving. Mary was a beautiful young black woman who already had three children. I was intrigued by her strong sense of herself and her culture. I had never been around black people before. My hometown consisted only of Mexicans, Native Americans, and Anglos.

I had moved to a large four-bedroom house. Twelve people lived in it. In the sixties and early seventies, communal living was quite popular. Sharing expenses and living together was perfect for me. I had become fearful of living alone. This living arrangement assured me that there would always be someone to come home to.

So there I was: living in a commune, working for a very successful hairdresser, assisting a beautiful and loving woman, and making fifteen dollars a day plus tips. I was thrilled. My only challenge was that I was still hitchhiking to work every day.

Nine months after I started working at the salon, my boss, Michael, gave me shocking news: he was leaving Arizona and moving to Texas to become a minister. Mary had left to have her baby, and I had successfully taken over her position. I was making good money and loved working with Michael. When he gave me the news about leaving, my heart sank. I thought my career was over. I felt like I was losing my best friend.

Michael was concerned about my hitchhiking, and before he left Phoenix he offered to help me find a car. He looked around and bought me a wonderful, but very used, Volkswagen Karmann Ghia. My first car! He also talked to the owner of the salon and suggested that I be given the chance to take his place as a master hairdresser. I was offered the opportunity, but I was scared. If I didn't keep at least half of Michael's clients, I would have to leave the salon. I thought to myself, "Is it ever easy, or do things like this happen to everyone?" Just when things are going well, change comes along, and it's not easy to accept.

I worked extremely hard to keep Michael's clients. I was inexperienced and slow, but I was determined to be successful. Within three months of Michael's departure, I was put on a commission base and was bringing in over two hundred dollars a day.

My hours were long and challenging, and the clients in the upscale salon were rich and demanding. For a naive small-town girl of only nineteen, the pressures were scary. When Mary was ready to return to work, I hired her. Now she was back at the salon and working for me! Her experience and assurance took some of my fear away.

I spent little time at the commune, which by now housed fifteen people. I didn't own anything except my car, and I worked most of the time, using the house only to sleep. One day as I pulled up to the house, I saw police cars, dogs, and handcuffed people being led away in vans. I should have known earlier that something was going on. After all, I was the only one with a real job, the only one who actually went to work every day. In those days almost everyone used drugs. It was a way of life for most "flower children," who were finding themselves and doing their own thing. My safe home was being busted for drug sales. I just kept on driving and never looked back. The next place where I lived I would be alone.

Two days after the drug bust I found a studio apartment in a great building. I had to work even harder to afford to live alone. I was very cautious about opening the door to anyone at any time of the day. As a matter of security, I would brace a chair under the doorknob before going to bed. To this day, when I travel I still perform this ritual before going to bed at night.

During the next year I visited my family occasionally. It was never easy to be home and experience my father again. I never stayed with them more than one night. I think that out of my desire to forget my childhood, I became inwardly distant from them. I would hug and kiss my mother and even my dad, but I felt angry and sad. I hated hearing the way he talked to Mom. I was glad to see that she was beginning to talk back and that she had stopped cowering from him. Many times I would encourage Mom to leave, telling her that she could come live with me in Phoenix. Truthfully, I would have had mixed feelings if she had done that. I wanted her to leave my father, but I also wanted to keep my freedom.

My older sister, Maggie, was married and gone from home. Carlos was in the Navy, married and a father, and was estranged from the family. My younger sister, Connie, had married at seventeen and had also left home. Going back was an obligation for me. I simply wanted to see Mom and make sure she was coping.

During the same year, while I was still nineteen, I began to hemorrhage severely each month. I had been a late bloomer and had not started my period until I was fourteen, which was late for our family. Even my little sister had been proud to beat me to it. Now, every month, I experienced ten to twelve days of excessive bleeding and excruciating pain.

One day, while I was working on a client, I passed out. When I came to, I was lying in a puddle of blood. I was so embarrassed that all I could do was cry. The client offered to take me to the hospital. I was weak from having lost much blood during the last few days, and standing all day on my feet hadn't helped.

In the emergency room the medics packed me to stop the bleeding and sent me back home. They also suggested I see a doctor as soon as possible, and since I did not have one, they recommended a Dr. Smith. A few days later I was in his office, relieved that I would finally get medical help. This painful monthly experience would soon be a thing of the past.

Dr. Smith was middle-aged, stocky, and blue-eyed. His manner was silent and distant. He said very little to me during the examination. When he was finished, he asked his nurse to leave the room. I was shocked at what came next. In a screeching voice he yelled, "Do you know what's wrong with you? The same thing that is wrong with all the girls just like you. You're just a bunch of whores! You sleep with anybody! There's nothing wrong with you that a good case of religion won't cure! You need Jesus in your life! God can heal everything! Now get out of here and find a church that will take someone as disgusting as you, and become saved!"

My mind flashed back to the priest who had slapped my friend while we were waiting for confession. We had been told that we were "sinners" since we were children. In spite of myself, I felt shame, guilt, and anger. So far, my relationship with God had been one of fear, fear and more fear. When I left Ajo, I vowed never to attend another church as long as I lived. It was too painful. I had kept that vow. Since I had moved to Phoenix, I had not attended any church service.

And here I was, lying naked and vulnerable in front of this doctor. I had nowhere to run. I wanted to call for help but did not know if anyone would even come. Who would care about me? Who knew the pain I had experienced? Who could even imagine it? Did everyone go through so much and was just unable to talk about it? I couldn't call my mother. She would worry, and she had enough to worry about. And my sister Maggie had her hands full with her own life. All of a sudden I felt totally alone. Maybe this doctor was right. I was disgusting. Maybe God was punishing me for all the thoughts I had about my father, wishing him dead.

The doctor left the room and I began to dress. I felt as if a car had hit me in my chest. I could barely move. Everything seemed to move in slow motion. I paid my bill and didn't look anyone in the face. I knew the nurses must have heard the doctor say those terrible things to me.

As I walked out of the office into the hall, my knees buckled. I fell to the floor, crying hysterically. I cried for all the times I couldn't cry before. I cried for my mother, for the life she was living. I cried for Maggie, for all the beatings she took and the tears she never cried for herself. I cried for our brother, who had not contacted the family in years, for what he had been through, for all the responsibility he had been given when he was still a boy. And I cried for our youngest sister, who no doubt had her own pain to deal with. I crouched on the floor, leaning against the wall, wishing again that I were dead.

I don't know how long I huddled there when I felt a pair of hands touch my shoulders. I looked up and saw a woman looking down at me.

"Are you OK?" she asked.

I told her honestly, "No." I wrapped my arms around her legs. "Please help me!"

I was desperate for someone to be with, someone who would care. The woman helped me up and took me to a room down the hall. She was an assistant to one of the doctors in the building. I told her what had happened, and she was shocked. She insisted that the doctor she worked for should see me. I didn't want to stay, yet I didn't want to leave, either. The woman waited with me until her doctor came in to see me. She stayed beside me the entire time, holding me in her arms and stroking my hair, just like Mom would have done if she had been with me.

Dr. Leo was a gentle man. He was very soft-spoken as he asked me about the bleeding, where I hurt, and how I took care of myself. He waited patiently for me to answer. I became conscious then of how little I knew about my body. Another checkup, another pair of hands touching me. I wanted to call out, "Touch me all you want, just take the pain away!" I was sore and tender and weak from loss of blood. Dr. Leo was not able to tell much from the simple checkup and was hesitant to dismiss me with just a Pap smear. But he had a gut feeling, and he made an appointment for me to get a biopsy at the outpatient clinic a week later. I felt relieved and actually looked forward to the appointment. I drove home, went to bed, and slept soundly.

The next day I began to worry about how I would get to the clinic. Dr. Leo had suggested that I not drive. I would be anesthetized, and driving afterwards was not recommended. Everyone I knew at the apartment house worked during the day, and I did not want to take a taxi. Hitchhiking was out of the question. I would ask my downstairs neighbor, Linda, for suggestions since she knew everyone who lived there.

The apartment house was a place where everyone knew everyone else. People worked hard during the day and partied hard at night and on weekends.

It was a wild bunch of young, professional people. They were generous, supportive, and helpful to each other. I had met everyone in the building on Sundays around the pool. That was the day to sun, drink, and then begin to sober up again for Monday.

Linda suggested that I talk to a neighbor named Clarence who lived downstairs from me. His father was very ill and in the hospital, and his mother was currently living with him in his tiny apartment. Clarence was going back and forth to the hospital with his mother, and the outpatient clinic was right across the street. This could work out very well!

I had met Clarence briefly at the pool one Sunday afternoon. He had gone through a difficult divorce and had made the decision to protect himself from being hurt again. He would never remarry and leave himself open to such pain. He was quiet and healthy. He did not smoke, drink, or use drugs and had been an avid weightlifter most of his life. I learned all this when I met him. I decided to ask him for a ride to the clinic.

He and his mother were having dinner at home before going to the hospital that evening. I apologized for interrupting and quickly asked him the critical question: Would he be able to drop me off at the clinic in the morning? He said he would, and we set a time to meet. This was great news. Now I only had to get a ride home afterwards, and I'd be all set.

Clarence drove me to the clinic and insisted on driving me home. I was very grateful and impressed that someone would be so nice to me, especially since he hardly knew me. I don't think the biopsy procedure took very long, but I do remember that Clarence was there, waiting.

On the way home, he talked to me about his dilemma with his mother, whose whole life depended on her husband. She had never learned to drive a car or to write checks to pay bills. She had not developed basic living skills. Her entire life had revolved around her home and her duties in it. Clarence was rightfully worried since he was the oldest of the three children. He felt fully responsible for his mother's wellbeing.

He talked of all this in a soothing voice. I was in and out, still groggy from the anaesthetic, partly sleeping and waking again. I didn't have much to say, so I just listened to his story and heard his pain. He helped me upstairs to my apartment. I thanked him and went to sleep.

Several days later, I received a call from the doctor's office. They wanted another biopsy. There were some questions about the results from the last one. We scheduled another appointment in two weeks. During this time I continued to work full-time. I also continued to have spotting and cramps.

I didn't see Clarence, but I heard from Linda that he was busy with his parents and his business, which required much traveling. His father was out of the hospital now and was also staying in the small studio, waiting for the doctors to let him leave Phoenix. His parents' home was in northern Arizona, a two-hour drive from Phoenix.

Once again I asked Clarence for a ride to the clinic, and again he agreed. He verified my checkout time and assured me he would be back. When I awoke, my doctor was there. I have always had a difficult time coming out of anesthesia. I have this feeling that I can't come back out. It is an anxious time where body and mind have yet to connect, and it seems forever until I can breathe again.

I will always remember the doctor's big brown eyes as he looked down at me and gave me the news: "You have cervical cancer." He must have said more, but I didn't hear him. I could see his mouth moving, feel his hand holding mine, but I heard nothing more until he said, "I've talked to your gentleman friend who's waiting to take you home, and he knows what we're going to do next." I was numb. Clarence took me home and I slept.

Whenever I awoke, he was there. He would give me pain pills, help me to the bathroom, and guide me back to bed. He fed me canned soup. It was

53

delicious. He told me stories of his childhood while I was awake, and he read to himself as I slept. I bled profusely and was very weak. This went on for about four days. I slept, rested, and listened. The stories of his childhood sounded wonderful to me. I wished my own childhood could have been so pleasant.

I didn't want to share my memories and my terror of what I had seen and experienced. This was not the time for it. All I wanted was to feel better. At nineteen years of age, I had lived a life of going from one crisis to another, including this one. I can honestly say, I thought this was normal.

For the next year and a half I was in and out of the hospital, having one surgery after another. I continued to work full-time, scheduling my doctor's appointments so I wouldn't have to miss much work. I was very busy at the salon and felt a great responsibility to the owner and to my clients, who had stayed with me. I seldom went home to visit my family during that time and never told them of my cancer. I didn't want Mom to worry.

Clarence and I continued to see each other and became friends. During the times when I felt better we would make love, but it was not really a sexual relationship. This was a relationship between two people in pain who needed mutual support and love. Clarence was a sad man. I was a needy woman, filled with a great desire to be connected to someone safe. On several occasions we talked about his past marriage. He had a son, now four years old, whom he saw on weekends. He was adamant that he would never marry again. He was sure that he could never trust anyone. This I completely understood.

One evening I began to hemorrhage again while I was with him at his apartment. We had been seeing each other for over two years. He rushed me to the emergency room. I was given a checkup and was shocked to hear the news that I was pregnant. I had been told that due to the cervical cancer and surgeries, my chances of having a child were minimal. I never expected such news!

The emergency room doctor kept me for a few hours, packed me and sent me home, suggesting that I see my own doctor as soon as possible. Clarence was waiting for me. He had been given the same news. When they wheeled me out of the examination room, I couldn't look at him, nor he at me. This was not in his plans. I could feel his sadness and frustration at the same time. We drove back home, neither one of us speaking a word to the other.

Joy is what I wanted to express. I wanted to yell at the top of my lungs, "I am going to have a miracle baby!" Instead, I buried my face in the pillow and cried myself to sleep. I didn't see Clarence for several days.

I called my mother and, as best as I could, brought her up to date on my circumstances. She wanted to know: How could I have allowed this to happen? Did I have any idea how Dad would react to this news? Did I really want to have this baby?

I knew in my heart that these questions were only a reaction coming from her fears. Mom loved children and was looking forward to Maggie's having a baby, Mom's first grandchild. Maggie was due in six months. Now I would have a baby in about seven months.

I know now that nothing happens by chance. And if it does, the only choice is to be creative. Life is but one creation after another. Every event, person, situation, and moment is an opportunity for us to remember who we truly are and to feel gratitude for life's never-ending opportunities to empower us. I would be having a baby! This would be the greatest relationship in my life.

My doctor and his partner suggested that I have a medical abortion. Their belief was that my pregnancy, by accelerating the growth of the uterus, would promote the spread of the cancer. In those days there was no way of testing to see if a fetus was healthy. I was taking an enormous chance in having this child, and they were not supportive of it. The repercussions of this pregnancy could be fatal for both the baby and me. Yet I could not terminate the pregnancy. My choice was to have this child. How do we make such life-changing choices? We do, we do it all the time.

Clarence did not want to marry me. It took me weeks to convince him that I couldn't have this child without a father. He finally agreed to marriage, but we would have it annulled as soon as I went back to work after the birth. The plan was that I would work until the time of delivery and get back to work as soon as possible. I promised to pay all the expenses and not ask him for help in any way. During this time, Clarence's father passed away of heart failure.

We drove to Las Vegas, Nevada, on August 1, 1971, and were married that same day. The minister was a tiny Italian man in a pinstriped blue suit. He looked like an actor in a movie. Several other couples were waiting in line for the seventy-five dollar wedding ceremony, music and flowers included. I wore the only nice suit that still fit me, a blue polyester pantsuit, which was now a bit tight around the waist. I paid for the ceremony.

Clarence spoke very little during our drive back. He was distant and quiet. My only thoughts were of changing him. I knew I could make him fall in love with me. We would move in together, and I would create a home for us filled with love. He would not be able to resist me and his new baby.

We did live together, but my new husband was seldom home. His traveling for business, his weightlifting, and the sports he loved left us very little time with each other.

After Clarence's father died, his mother became dependent on us for nearly everything. Because of his father's long-term illness and his mother's inability to take care of their bills, his father's life insurance policy was cancelled without notification. There was no money left to care for her, and she was only fifty-six years old.

She lived in an apartment not far from us and found a housekeeping job at a nearby resort. A group of women formed a carpool and, for a small amount of money, drove her to and from work every day. Weekends, holidays and anything else that required driving became my responsibility. Marge was not fond of me. The age difference of fourteen years between Clarence and me, and the fact that I had become pregnant before getting married, upset her.

Little Bolts of Light

During my years of cervical cancer, I never gave up hope that some miracle would come into my life. My child came to me then. All I can say is never, never, never give up.

Affirmation:

**I never give up, and
I expect a miracle.**

My Son Ron

My pregnancy was very difficult. I experienced morning sickness for six months. Every morning I awoke exhausted from lack of sleep and nausea. I had constant heartburn, swollen legs and feet, and sore, tender breasts. Somehow I managed to eat constantly. It seemed to keep the nausea down if I had something in my stomach. In nine months I gained over fifty pounds; I was the heaviest I had ever been in my life. Considering that I have a petite frame and very thin legs, I was a sight to behold.

I had always heard that pregnant women look beautiful, that they have an inner glow. This was not my experience. I was huge and uncomfortable, not beautiful or glowing! Most of all, I wanted to be held and loved and comforted, none of which I was getting at home. I longingly observed other couples where the father-to-be caressed the mother's belly, showing his love for her and his desire to be part of the birth experience. Since these expressions of love were not available to me in my marriage, I buried myself in work and allowed my clients at the salon to love me and touch me.

I attended natural childbirth classes by myself in preparation for delivery. My nine months seemed like forever. I worked full-time up to the last moment. On the morning of February 26, 1972, I woke up in a wet bed. My husband was asleep next to me. I quietly pulled myself out of bed, trying not to wake him, which was not easy for a 175-pound pregnant woman. I worried how I would tell him that I had wet the bed, and that he was lying in it.

I was in the kitchen having a cup of hot tea when Clarence came in and said, "Your water broke."

"I don't know," I answered, feeling terribly stupid. How could I not have figured this out myself? I had expected pain or cramping but had felt nothing. After a phone call to the doctor, we were on our way to the hospital.

By noon nothing had happened, so I was given medication into my bloodstream. By one p.m. I was finally in labor, and just a few hours later, our son was born. He weighed in at eight pounds nine ounces, and was twenty-two-and-a-half inches long. He was the most beautiful baby I had ever seen, and he was in perfect health! He had all his fingers, and all his toes. I slowly went over every

inch of this little body and marveled at the perfection
I held in my arms.

Birth is one of those special moments in life when
one never forgets the time, place, or words spoken.
I still hear the words ringing in my ears as the
doctor and two nurses said, "It's a boy! A big boy!
He looks healthy!" I still feel joy and relief, and I
am flooded with gratitude as I recall this moment.
I wanted this child more than I valued my own
life. I used to wonder where such a deep desire
comes from. And now it doesn't matter, it's just
there.

Clarence and I had talked about people and places
and things, but I do not remember that we made
any plans for the baby. I am not sure we ever
communicated about him before his birth.
Clarence never asked me how I felt, whether I
needed or wanted something, or what we should
name the baby. It was strange when the nurse
asked for a name and I had to answer, "We haven't
decided on a name yet." I was very embarrassed. I
wanted to pretend that my husband and I were
very close and that we loved each other immensely,
but I couldn't. I truly didn't know how he felt, or
by now, how I felt.

These thoughts and feelings I now know to be
clues, pieces of information that do not seem to fit
into our lives. But here they are, and we must do
something with them. Sometimes we pretend they

do not bother us. Other times we admit that they hurt, but we dismiss them. These clues are like steps that lead us to our next level of understanding and raise the question: Is this what I want my life to be, and where am I going with it?

I had bought a new Bentwood rocking chair, which stood facing a window in the living room of our small apartment. The view was not glorious, just the apartments across the walkway, but if you looked hard to your right, you could see a tree and a bit of lawn. This would have to be my view for now. I was looking forward to being home, rocking my baby.

I stayed in the hospital for two nights. My mother was ill and was not able to help me, and neither was Clarence's mother. I was going to be alone with my baby and my husband.

When we arrived home, Clarence put my overnight case in the bedroom and informed me that he was leaving for the day. He had to attend a baseball playoff game. As the door closed behind him, I wondered if this would be my fate for the rest of my life. I sat in the rocker, holding my baby close to my heart. His soft little lips were up against my neck, and his wild black mop of hair tickled my chin. My sweet, precious little son! Did every new mother feel like this? Was every woman thrilled and afraid at the same time?

I laid him on my lap, marveling at his perfect body. He was beautiful. What would the future hold for us? Would I be able to raise him alone? The thought of being alone filled me with fear, and I began to cry uncontrollably.

It seemed as if we sat for hours together in our rocker. I would cry, and then he would cry, then we would stop, and together we would cry some more. There was so much to think about. I needed to make plans. The doctors had already suggested that I have a hysterectomy, fearing that the pregnancy may have spread the cancer.

Then my thoughts turned to guilt. Had I made the right decision? Should I have had this child? What if there was something wrong with him? What if I had the next surgery and did not survive? Who would take care of my son and raise him? Did Clarence feel trapped? Did he have any feelings of love for me at all? He had never actually said "I love you" to me.

Clarence had turned on the radio before he left, and now it caught my attention. I heard Paul Harvey delivering his well known "The Rest of the Story" program. He talked about a family with nine children that lived on a small mid-western farm. The oldest son had proudly received his driver's license that week and asked his father if he could take the family station wagon into town, just a few miles up the road. The father agreed and suggested he take all the children along with him for a ride. On their way back home, the car stalled on the railroad tracks. An oncoming train hit the car and all nine children were killed.

Did I really hear this story? Maybe I had fallen asleep sitting in the rocker. Had I been dreaming? As I continued to listen, Paul Harvey spoke about how this shocking incident would dramatically change the lives of so many, especially the parents who had lost their nine children.

I had indeed heard the story, and it had come at a perfect time. My heart needed this jolt. I needed to get a perspective on what was important to move me out of my negative thinking. I had made a conscious choice to have this child. In my arms I held this new life, my son. I clearly remember my thoughts shifting. It didn't matter if my husband would or could ever love me. I had just received a miracle, the gift of my child. We named him Ron.

The cancer had spread into my uterus. The doctors tried to stop the bleeding and get me strong enough to have a hysterectomy.

However, during that waiting period, little Ron needed major surgery. A large tumor on his left forearm was restricting his movements and growth. The possibility of a malignancy would call for the removal of his arm. The surgery lasted several hours. Clarence and I sat in the waiting room, numb to each other. I caught a glimpse of the doctor walking toward us and my heart stopped. The tumor was benign, he said. Ron kept his arm, and I continued to bleed.

Two months later, at the age of twenty-two, I had a hysterectomy. I spent a month in the hospital because of complications. I had hired a wonderful woman, a distant cousin from Mexico, to stay at the apartment and care for Ron and Clarence. Within another month I was back at work in the salon to pay off all the medical bills that Ron and I had incurred.

The following year we moved into a small, three-bedroom home. Clarence and I had ignored our agreement to divorce after the baby came. It seemed as if we were just going from one crisis to the next. I was still hopeful that our marriage would work, but neither he nor I ever talked about it, and I pretended to have forgotten our agreement to divorce after the birth of the baby.

Clarence's mother, Marge, was diagnosed with terminal cervical cancer and was given six months to live. At my suggestion she moved in with us. I would take care of her as evidence of my appreciation for Clarence marrying me when I needed a father for my son. Those were my sincere thoughts. I was so grateful that he married me that I wanted to repay him. Marge moved in with us and occupied the third bedroom, which was also

Clarence's office. At first her health deteriorated, but then she stabilized.

My schedule was challenging. Even with a small child, I worked at the salon three to four days a week. I was up early to prepare breakfast for our one-year old toddler and for Marge, who always enjoyed eating. I bathed her every other day. She weighed no more than seventy-five pounds. Small as I was, I would lift her in my arms and take her into the shower with me. I scrubbed her, dried her off, put clean pajamas on her, tucked her into bed, and left for work. I came home at lunch, fed her, went back to work, picked up Ron from the nursery, made dinner for us, cleaned, and got ready for another day.

Clarence could not handle his mother's illness and was gone most of the time. Marge continued to live with us, dying slowly, for over two years. This was my life in my mid-twenties: a lonely existence, disconnected from my husband, and fearful at home with a mother-in-law who resented me and would often tell me so. Marge had two other children, both younger than Clarence, a daughter and a son. Neither one helped us with her. They were busy with their own lives.

I now know that Clarence was depressed. My desire to be loved and feel safe kept me with him for six years. His age, his calm, quiet disposition, and the love which he developed over time for our son got me through this difficult period in our lives.

But though I was coping, I was developing some neurotic behaviors. One was an obsession with cleaning. I would spend hours scrubbing and scouring the house with such intensity and dysfunctional attention to detail that I couldn't sleep for days. Another obsession became my inability to eat solid food. I began to starve myself. Slowly and surely, I was on the way to ending my life. I was given Valium for this condition. Thus passed six years in a lonely, quiet existence with a man who never shared himself with me emotionally, a man I called my husband, the father of my son.

Little Bolts of Light

Nothing sustains us like a deep sense of gratitude. I lived because of my strong desire to repay a favor. And I was extremely grateful for the birth of my son. The only way I knew to show my gratitude was to give myself up. How better to get in touch with all that you are than by losing yourself first? Now I know that I do not have to give up the self. I can integrate the power of gratitude and use it as a magical energy and an instrument of healing. Gratitude, the great healer.

Affirmation:

Gratitude sustains and heals me.

Seven

Birthing My Spirituality

Whaten I told Clarence that I wanted a divorce, he was stunned. He had no idea that I was unhappy. He did not want a divorce and said that he would not sign the papers. He had a strong bond with our son and did not want to separate from him. After a year we did divorce, but not without painful emotional incidents that took a toll on all of us, including our son. During this time I began to feel strength within myself. Little by little, I was learning to ask for what I wanted.

I had been divorced a year when I married Jerry. My new husband was talented, charismatic, and energetic. He was also an alcoholic. In my naivete and unending desire to feel loved, safe and secure, I avoided seeing his greatest secret: he was manic-depressive.

The excitement that surrounds a man like this drew me in at first like a moth to the flame. I felt as if I were in a trance. I was desperate to be touched and cared for. Jerry's charm was magnetic. He was worldly and wonderful with people. He was everything I wanted to be and was too insecure to become. Over the protests of my mother, who sensed trouble with this man, I married him.

His manic-depressive illness controlled our relationship. We were all on a roller coaster. It was a frightening ride, with no seat belts to hold me or my son. We were thrown from one crisis to the next. I felt terror again, a terror that was familiar — it was my childhood all over again. Jerry's public displays of verbal abuse, contrasted with lavish, extravagant gifts, were crazy-making. During his highs, he was financially successful, personable, and controlled. During his lows, he was in debt, verbally abusive, and totally out of control. Which one was my real husband? At the same time, I wondered if the real me would ever show up.

Jerry's relationship with my son Ron was intense. Until we were married, Jerry had worked at developing a friendship with him. When we married, Ron was six years old, very bright, artistically talented, and a dedicated bookworm. He spent hours in his room drawing, sketching and reading. But this was not the kind of son Jerry wanted. He would have preferred a ball-playing, roughhousing, aggressive youngster, and he never missed an opportunity to let Ron know his preferences. Ron struggled to change in order to be accepted by his step-father. It was difficult for him and painful for me to witness Jerry's attacks. Over and over again, Jerry would let me know all the things that he thought were wrong with Ron and, of course, I blamed myself. I doubted how I was raising my son and wondered if Jerry was right. As a mother, I was confused and torn between my husband's opinions and my own inherent knowing of who my son was and what was right for him.

Seven years into our marriage, Jerry and I bought a new home. We had separated twice before but had returned to each other with promises to work things out. We thought a new neighborhood and a bigger, better home would help our marriage. The house was a two-story Santa Fe style. Downstairs were a large master bedroom, a bath, huge closets, a formal living room and formal dining room, a family room, kitchen, breakfast area, two fire places, and a powder room. Upstairs were two bedrooms, a library, and a large bathroom. This beautiful house was a dream come true for this little Mexican girl from Ajo.

My mother came to help us on moving day. Her room was upstairs next to Ron's. We had worked all day with the movers and the housekeeper to get settled, and we were exhausted from a long day of labor. It was after midnight when we finished. I walked through the entire house once more to make sure everything was locked and secure. Everything was ready, and I could turn in.

Jerry had gone to bed earlier and was already

asleep. As my head hit the pillow, I thought of the possibilities for our marriage. Maybe we could work out our differences in raising Ron. Just maybe the money issue would settle into a steady stream instead of all the highs and lows. The list in my mind went on and on. As I lay there with my eyes closed, thinking of these things, I sensed someone looking at me.

I opened my eyes in the dark and looked toward the double doors that opened to the living room. There, in the open doorway, stood three women, looking at me. I sat up and screamed, grabbing Jerry's arm at the same time. He was startled and jumped out of bed, trying to get his bearings.

"What is it?" he yelled.

"Three women!" I yelled back. "Standing in the doorway!"

He turned on the lights. We searched the house and yard and found nothing.

The appearance of the three women continued for weeks, no matter what time I went to bed. At first Jerry tried to tell me the appearances weren't real, then he checked into the property's history. Had there been a burial ground here? He searched for any answer to this nightly visitation, but he could find none. He had his doubts, but nothing could convince me that this wasn't happening. I knew it was real.

The women, whose faces I could not make out, were large. They were dressed in traditional Native American clothing. Their heads and faces were covered. Every night, without fail, they were there. Jerry made me promise not to tell anyone about this. People would think I was crazy.

Week after week this evening ritual continued until I became rather comfortable with it. I actually got to the point where I looked forward to seeing the women. Something was beginning to tell me that this was safe and that some day I would be able to understand their appearances.

I still worked long hours at the salon, and the challenges of running a new home kept me very busy. Jerry and I continued to have problems. The only part of my life that seemed secure and reliable was the visit of the three women who came to see me every night. We never communicated; we just acknowledged each other through our thoughts. At least I sensed that they were able to read my thoughts.

Five months later, Jerry and I separated again. He moved out of the house. That evening the three women appeared, and if you can just follow me with this, I would like to describe a most wondrous light show: Three women are standing in the doorway. They turn into three balls of purple, red, and blue lights. They move through the room fast, leaving a trail of sparkling silver stars like snowflakes that evaporate in the air. More lights come from the walls and the ceiling and some from under the bed. The room is filled with bright lights, dancing everywhere. I am lying in bed witnessing this light show. I am not afraid. All this feels quite natural.

This magnificent sight was a sign to me that somehow everything would be all right. I was not now, nor would I ever be, alone. The experience went on for several minutes. When it was over, I simply fell asleep. I felt cleansed and assured and connected with something.

I did not share this experience with anyone, fearing that people would think I had gone off the deep end. I must admit that my logical left brain could not make any sense of this light display, but my intuitive right brain kept insisting that it was not necessary for me to believe it or understand it. I know what I saw and what I experienced.

Are there things beyond our five senses that we cannot yet see or feel or hear or touch? Are things out there, just waiting for the perfect moment to show up? I say yes, I am here to tell you that I have seen it, felt it, touched it, heard it and tasted it, this other side of "real," the infinite side of creation. I recall my own childhood near-death experience in the hospital and the spirit of Delfina, the woman who had been dead for two years and whose spirit still walked the earth. Nothing could shake my belief that the other side exists. My only questions were, why now? and what was I to do with this?

Jerry and I were separated for about a year. During this time he moved back in to the house and I moved out. We dated each other and we dated others. Our continuing attraction to each other and our addiction for each other created anger and constant confusion. What was it that I couldn't understand? What was my life with this man all about?

Although I was having beautiful mystical experiences, my energy and focus were on my fear of being alone, of being abandoned, of losing everything I had worked so hard for. "For the thing which I greatly feared is come upon me, and that which I was afraid of is come to me." (Job 3:25) I know now that what we fear we attract to us like a magnet.

I moved back in with Jerry during my birthday month a year later. We were determined to make the marriage work. By now we had been together for almost nine years. I knew it was up to me. I needed to change my thinking and accept him as he was. We had lived a life of material wealth. We had traveled, entertained, and bought the most expensive toys money could buy. What we didn't have was a healthy emotional and spiritual foundation.

I had shared with Jerry the stories of my difficult

childhood and the financial and emotional poverty that we had endured growing up. He wanted to make up for this by giving me everything materially, and although I loved it, I struggled with the guilt of having too much. My family had little money, and I felt uncomfortable with all I had. In coming back to him I wanted us to work on developing our spiritual and emotional health. I shared with him my desire to develop spiritually. This did not go over well with him. He said I had gone crazy. He didn't know who I was any longer.

Unbeknown to me, during our year of separation, Jerry had not made house payments for several months. Our beautiful house was now being repossessed by the bank. A ten-thousand-dollar lien on my car was due. Our credit cards were all at their maximum, and there was a note for sixty-five thousand dollars at the bank in Jerry's name. And to make matters even more challenging, Jerry had not filed income taxes for two years. We owed money to the IRS.

We decided to file for a divorce six weeks after I moved back in. Jerry told me the whole story of our financial mess as we were discussing the divorce. Since we lived in Arizona, a community property state, I was equally liable for the debt. Jerry was moving away from Arizona and would leave me with all of this to handle. This was the man who for years had said to me, "Trust me, I will never hurt you." And here he was now, looking at me across the kitchen table, saying, "I am leaving you and your son. You are so strong that you can take care of this yourself."

And that is exactly what I did. I filed for divorce, and, on the advice of my attorney, I also filed for bankruptcy. I paid off the lien against my car and a couple of the credit cards. The IRS garnisheed my wages and gave me an allowance to live on. My home was gone. I sold everything I could to pay off personal bills, the IRS, and attorneys' fees.

During this time I became very ill again. I developed skin cancer and severe food allergies. I had been eating only limited foods to begin with, so this was terrible news. I also developed severe anxiety and panic attacks. My body felt assaulted. I felt defeated and forsaken. Where was the God of love and for-giveness? Did I need or want to be forgiven for something? My Catholic background convinced me that I was being punished for something I had done and that, no doubt, I must deserve this punishment.

The divorce took over a year. Jerry was living in Florida near his parents. I knew he was in trouble, but I could only take care of myself and my son. My reactions to his accusations of my not being there for him and not supporting him kept me in a state of guilt and depression. I didn't know who I was or what would make me feel better.

The anxiety attacks became more severe and more frequent. I could not connect with God, so I could not develop a relationship with my spiritual self. I was afraid of this God who was punishing me so. I ached for the love of God and at the same time, out of fear, I pushed the love away. As much as I prayed, I didn't believe I deserved to be happy. I didn't know what happy felt like.

The three women continued to show up every night, but I would turn away and cover my face. I was ashamed and felt distant from them. Night after night they came. Immersed in my pain, I could not extend my energy to connect or to reach out.

Little Bolts of Light

How fortunate I was to have not just one but three angels with me! I know now that they represented the trinity: Body, Mind and Spirit. But I was so focused on my new home and my expectations for improving my marriage that I could not give my spiritual self the attention it wanted. How many times do our expectations get in the way of a discovery? We become consumed by what we think "should be" and leave no room for "what is." This is the secret: accept the fruits of the present, whatever they are.

Affirmation:

The present moment is my greatest gift.

Eight

A Turning Point

At the age of thirty-six I went mad. I am talking about the kind of madness that occurs when your thoughts take you to a place where you don't want to go. The madness that comes when you can no longer make sense of anything and you are not sure if you will come out of it alive. The madness that occurs when you want to avoid your family and closest friends just when you need them most. The senseless madness that makes you want to die. Scared to death, I pleaded for help to someone or something I wasn't sure even existed.

The thought of being alone brought increasing terror into my life. I was experiencing panic attacks to the point where I no longer trusted myself to drive a car. A few times when I was driving, I became so overwhelmed with fear that I pulled off the road, knocked on a stranger's door, and asked the person to just hold me. This condition became so bad that someone had to drive me to and from the salon every day. I could not eat. I kept myself alive on juices and water.

My life was full of responsibilities. I was now running the salon, which had thirty employees, and I was dealing with severe personal financial challenges. Yet I could not make even the simplest decisions.

One evening as I sat alone, I began to doubt that any of my prayers would ever be answered. My son was away for the weekend with his father. Christmas was only a week away. I sat at the edge of my bed for what seemed like hours. I prayed, then I doubted. I prayed, then I feared. I visited my childhood and teenage memories and struggled with them while also desperately wanting to suppress them.

In his book, *My Ending Is My Beginning*, David Rankin writes: "To make an ending is to make a beginning. This end is where we start from." I sat alone, thinking only of ending. I was defeated and exhausted and ready to leave this life experience behind me. In my hand I held a bottle of tranquilizers, my doctor's prescription for whatever it was that was wrong with me. I had never forgotten hovering over my body at the age of six. At that moment I longed to be there again. I swallowed the entire contents of the bottle.

It was almost over. I had lost all my battles, and now I was ready to end my war. I had a great yearning to go "home." I prayed that my son, who was fourteen, would somehow understand, that he would not blame me or resent me for leaving. I had raised him to be independent, loving and strong, all the attributes I so longed for as a child and even now, as an adult. I missed him already as I lay there and thought of what I had just done. My mind clouded with softness, and I began to drift into a welcoming sleep. I hoped my son would read the letter I had written him and that he would love me and forgive me.

As I drifted, I saw a woman standing by my bed. She was dressed in a soft purple robe. She came to me, sang to me, and whispered sweet and wonderful delights to me. She sat down beside me and assured me that all would be well. She stroked me and held me, just as my mother had done during my most frightening childhood times.

Was she an angel sent to me? Her presence filled me with love. She talked to me and told me stories, yet she never uttered a sound. I felt a deep connection to her in my heart. I drifted deeper and higher at the same time. She held me and loved me and comforted me throughout this dream. I saw people's faces and visited places I had long ago forgotten. I was a child, laughing and playing. This couldn't happen to me. I was missing the familiar feeling of terror! She held me and loved me during the night. She assured me that she would never leave me and that I would, in fact, some day be free.

Some time during the evening I came to realize

that this beautiful angel was one of the three women who had been my nightly visitors in our new house. She was part of the light show in the evenings after Jerry left. I had not seen the women for a long time, and now one of them was with me. She would become my guide, my dearest friend. I would never be alone again. A year later I would learn her name.

Some time before sunrise, I awoke. I was alive! I had been given a gift, the gift of my own life! I lay there exhausted, trembling with joy. I was filled with overwhelming gratitude. If I had been able to move I would have jumped and cheered, but I could only lie there. I stayed in bed for two days, feeling a transformation developing within me.

Lying there, I made promises to God and to myself. Now I knew that the God I had longed for had been with me the entire time. I had never been alone after all. Just as I knew before I was born that I was afraid, I now knew beyond doubt that my life was going to change. I also knew that I was the only one who could make this change happen. This near-death experience was the catalyst toward the healing that I so desperately desired.

My prayers now focused on finding wisdom, guidance and strength. I knew it wouldn't be easy or fast, but I was committed and determined to become consciously alive for the first time in my life. God became my partner, and I set out to discover my true and whole self. And so I began my journey on the other side of fear.

One beautiful person after another came into my life then with words, books, love, and suggestions that I could follow. I was introduced to holistic medicine, a system of healthcare which emphasizes personal responsibility and the attunement of body, mind, emotions and spirit. At the time this was a new concept in the healing arena. And at times I was doubtful, but I was also excited. I felt I had nothing to lose and everything to gain. This is where my real work in achieving health began. I would begin to meet all of me.

The most important piece in the puzzle of self-healing came with Dr. John Reed, a holistic medical doctor. My first visit to him was the second catalyst that changed my life. During that visit, Dr. Reed looked at me for several moments, stood up, walked around me and said, "What do you eat, and do you like to eat?" No doctor had ever asked me that, and I certainly was not prepared for his second question, "How long has it been since you've cried?"

I began to talk. My story about my eating habits poured out. It had been months since I had eaten solid foods. I had hidden in my home and avoided social functions as much as possible. When I did find myself at a dinner table with others, I would move my food around my plate and hide food in my napkin. The truth was, I could not put food in my mouth without having an anxiety attack. The fear of choking would overcome me and I would vomit.

Over the years, several doctors had prescribed Valium for my anxiety attacks. When Ron was small, one advised me to quit my job and stay home with my baby. In time, as a housewife, I would get over this "eating thing" that was bothering me, he said. I had been on liquids, hiding, occasionally taking Valium, and keeping my secret to myself for almost twelve years. There were times, though, when I could eat, and during those times I ate as if I might never eat again. My family had questioned my eating habits, joking and making fun of me. How I wanted to share with them what I was feeling and the torture I was going through! I could not remember when I had ever really enjoyed eating.

Considering that I had spent my entire childhood crying, and had comforted myself during my early adult years with tears, I now couldn't remember when I had cried the last time. "I don't cry any more," I answered. Just the sound of those words sent chills down my back. I became aware that I had consciously stopped crying.

Dr. Reed took my hand, sat down facing me, and said, "Go ahead and cry." What was he doing? I thought. He said again, "Go ahead and cry now." And I did, sobbing for a long time. He kept encouraging me to do so, and it felt good. I felt as if I could begin all over again. Through my tears I was releasing the old me and preparing to rebuild a new me. He held me as if I were a child. He cradled me in a safe and loving way. I had never been treated so respectfully by a doctor in my life. He assured me that it was appropriate for me to call out my tears. And this I did. I called out my tears. The longer I cried the more parts of my body came alive. I had been numb in places that I had purposefully shut off to protect myself.

This is what I needed, someone who could introduce me to me. Dr. Reed gave me a new definition for my physical body. I learned that it is a living organism with needs and desires I had not honored before. After that visit with him, I began to listen to my body's messages for the first time. I developed a partnership with it that began to consist of healthy food, rest, and appropriate exercise. What a concept! You would have thought I had never heard any of this before. "When the student is ready, the teacher appears," is an ancient saying that applied to me at that time.

In spite of my eating disorder and constant health challenges, I had been a runner for many years, and had even completed a marathon. I continued to run as if I were training for another twenty-six mile race. But I knew something had to change. Instead of pushing myself to my limits, I decided to slow down, to jog more often, and to walk as my new exercise. I actually became comfortable in allowing someone to pass me while I was jogging or walking. I did not feel the strong need to compete that I had before or to prove how fast I was. This was a first.

I started acupuncture to relax me and get me off the Valium, which I had become dependent on. Slowly, my desire for food appeared, and patiently and lovingly I began to enjoy the simple act of eating. Eating a normal diet was a great challenge and yet a most rewarding part of my healing. I tested highly sensitive to wheat, yeast, dairy, sugar, preservatives, several vegetables, caffeine, and many other foods. I can't remember all of them any longer. I will always remember that first mouthful of wonderful solid food. To this day I take a moment to be consciously grateful before each meal. For those of you who are able to relate to this eating challenge, I know how you feel.

"What do you think about?" Dr. Reed asked me on one of my visits.

"What everyone thinks about," I answered.

Dr. Reed enlightened me on the power of the mind. "What you think about, you create."

He gave me a few instructions to follow: "Turn off your television and your radio. Don't listen to music with words. Just listen to soft, gentle piano melodies for now and pay attention to what you are thinking. Begin to consciously direct and control what comes and goes in your thoughts. Meditate and pray. Pray with gratitude and affirm your health. Use the power of your mind to see yourself well. Slow down. You have plenty of time to do all and be all you want."

These suggestions have been the most powerful tools ever given to me.

So much opened up for me during that first year of learning to live on the other side of fear. My greatest desires had been to feel safe, whole, and connected. I began to see that this was an inside job. It had to come from within me before I could create it on the outside.

It did not come to me quickly. I began with very small steps. Consciously, I began paying attention to every thought I had. I paid attention to each word I said, and I became acutely aware of my environment and the people I allowed in it.

During this time I had very little contact with my family. My mother had divorced our dad after thirty-two years of marriage. My relationship with her was loving but distant. We would talk by phone about once a week. Sometimes she would come from Ajo and stay overnight, but a new job and a new man in her life kept her busy, and she was not available for sharing herself much.

Later on I would work on my issues with my mother. I would come to develop a deep, strong love for her and for her commitment to raising us and not leaving her abusive marriage until we were all on our own. I learned to respect her and appreciate her desire to provide a family life for us while we were growing up. She compromised herself for what she believed was best for her children. She loved us more than she loved herself. I am not suggesting this was right. On the other hand, who am I to say she was wrong?

I began to learn not to avoid my fears but to dance with them. To embrace my most frightening thoughts and see through them. I wanted a life of health and joy. I really wanted to LIVE, and I could now see myself creating this reality. After all, I was now driving my car and eating real food again. Most importantly, the secrets I had been hiding were no longer controlling me.

I learned that I wasn't alone. Dr. Reed brought me to the understanding that there are many people, especially women, just like me. He told me there are others who keep their secrets buried. Unfortunately, they can be eaten alive by them. His work with me connected me to the world. It became a place I no longer wanted to fear.

Next, my dear doctor suggested that I go into counseling to help heal my fractured feelings and beliefs. I replied that I was sure a couple of months would do. I interviewed three therapists. The third woman I saw was Dr. Marilyn Powers. I sat across from her and gave her the same information: a couple of months would be enough for this. She smiled and assured me that we would both know when I was ready to stop therapy and be on my way.

I spent the next three years in intensive therapy. I am eternally grateful for the enlightening life-changing process that I experienced under the guidance of Marilyn and her husband, Dr. Frank Powers. Revisiting my childhood was my biggest challenge. Over and over again, I relived those moments of intense fear and anger. I had lost my childhood and fled into the comfort of illness. I learned that if I was physically ill, I could avoid my emotional fears. Slowly the pieces of the puzzle of my life came together.

Dr. Reed insisted that I reintroduce myself to God. He was adamant. "Without a belief in a loving God, there will not be a healing." The keyword here was *loving*. I had never thought of God as loving. The God I knew was fearsome, punishing, and far away. Even though I prayed often I had not yet developed a relationship with God. I had prayed and felt connected to my angel. I had prayed to calm myself out of anxious moments, and she was there. I had prayed to give myself hope, and I could feel her presence. Now I would pray for guidance and wisdom in developing a relationship with God.

I also began to pray for a perfect church that would meet my spiritual needs. I attended many different churches but did not connect with any of them. Finally, at thirty-seven years of age, I found my spiritual home with the Science of Mind philosophy at the Church of Religious Science. Science of Mind is a philosophy, a faith, a way of life. I became a student and welcomed the teachings of the Power of Mind, our mind, the One Mind of an infinite, loving God. Through this church I moved farther along on my journey from dark to light, from fear to love. I embraced the spirit-filled life, that of the seeker, the lover, and the creator. This philosophy would change my being forever. Thank you, sweet giver of life!

Little Bolts of Light

A loving relationship with our self brings us to the most important relationship we will ever have in our lifetime: the relationship with God.

Affirmation:

**The most important
relationship I have
is my relationship with God.**

Nine

My Spiritual Journey

$\mathcal{I}$ was taking charge of my life, continuing my
emotional counseling, and becoming immersed in
the teachings of the Science of Mind philosophy.
During this time I was also introduced to a group
called "Values Realization," led by Dr. Sid Simon. His
workshops offer opportunities for empowerment
and networking. People use values principles to
positively impact the quality of their life. I attended
my first Sid Simon workshop in July of 1989. I
enjoyed the power of the group and found myself
contributing easily to it. I loved speaking! Through
this experience I realized that I wanted to develop
and lead my own workshops. I desired to work
with groups, even as I was on my own journey of
healing.

My intention was clear: I had a passionate desire to
help others in discovering themselves and reclaiming
their lives. The following January I presented my
first workshop, "A Healing Journey: a Spiritual
Awakening for Women." No doubt my gratitude
for my own healing process inspired me to begin
there. I wanted my work to reflect both the spiritual

insights of Science of Mind and the empowering concepts taught by Dr. Simon. I could feel myself claiming my own unique life. I was learning who I was.

I spent most of my time reading, writing, and in deep meditative prayer. My beautiful angel, who had been with me during my darkest night, became my constant companion. In my dreams she shared with me stories of magical places and mystical times. She showed me colors and sounds I had never experienced before. She shared with me journeys of times yet to come. During the day I could feel her presence around me. At times she was inside me, and we became one. I still did not know her name, and I often wondered about it.

One day while I was working in the salon on a client, I had a great desire to share the story of my angel with her. I had not talked to anyone about her presence before; she was now my most precious secret. As I told my client about my angel, she lit up. Her entire being was delighted with my story. I told her about my desire to know my angel's name.

"Do you know that I know how to communicate with these entities?" she asked.

"No," I answered, "I have no idea why I even shared this story with you. I just felt directed to do it."

"You will see," she said to me.

She suggested that at exactly ten o'clock that evening, I should prepare for my angel. She gave me very specific instructions on how to set up a small table with dried lavender leaves, a candle, and the figurine of an angel. I was to prepare for bed as usual and pray for this communication to happen. In the past I had not asked for her to come; she had appeared on her own.

At ten that evening I was ready. I had stopped at a bookstore where I could buy what I needed. My angel figurine, dried lavender, and a beautiful scented candle were set up on my little altar. I was full of prayers of gratitude for this evening and affirmed that I would know the name of my angel before the night was over. As I knelt in prayer, I felt as if I was being born again, as if my whole being was another person. I felt as if I could be born over and over again, only bigger and more awakened to the Self each time. The room was still and dark. The candle light flickered on the walls and ceiling. I felt my angel's presence, and I heard her name very clearly. From then on I would call her by her name, Emma.

I called my client the next day and thanked her for her help. She assured me that this was her purpose, to help others discover the other side. As the months went on, though, I began to question that evening and Emma's name. I wanted to discuss her with more people. I wanted to know that I wasn't imagining this.

Part of my healing journey, as recommended by Dr. Reed, was to have my body worked on as well as my mind and soul. To do that, I saw Sandy once a week for acupressure treatments. I had never mentioned my angel story to Sandy. One morning when I arrived at her house, she greeted me with great excitement.

"Come in and see what I was told to do for you today," she said.

When I entered her healing room I looked with amazement. There at the head of the massage table was a smaller table set with dried lavender leaves, a candle, and the small figurine of an angel.

"Who told you to do this?" I asked.

"I just felt it this morning when I woke up. It seemed as if it was what I needed to do for you today." We hugged and laughed and decided that this was perfect. I did not mention my story of Emma to her.

Sandy left the room. I undressed and lay face down on the table, ready for my hour-long treatment, a very worthwhile hour which helped me on my road to recovery. I couldn't help but wonder how she knew the table set-up for calling in my angel's name. Sandy came back in, and as she put her big warm hands on my back, I felt something very unusual. I felt as if she was not actually touching me, but that she was touching someone lying on top of me. I felt Sandy's hands through this etheric, nonphysical body. The stillness and quiet was eerie. I tried to figure out what was going on while Sandy held her hands in the same place.

She finally broke the spell and asked, "Hilda, who is here?"

"Emma," I replied.

She worked on me for an hour, and we never spoke another word. I knew Sandy was getting to know Emma through me. I knew they were sharing information. I could feel my energy growing. I felt that everything was in slow motion, as if hours had passed. I smelled the lavender and the candle as if they were far, far away. I heard music as if I were traveling from one dimension of life to another. I saw colors and felt them penetrating my body and soul. I felt sensitive to every touch from Sandy's hands that had yet to touch my own body directly. She was still working through the vibration of my angel.

For the entire hour I was in another dimension. With every breath I felt as if I were letting go of more of the old self, breathing in more of my Emma. Sandy and I didn't need to talk afterwards.

She knew, and I knew that she knew. She had experienced Emma. Several weeks later I wrote the following poem:

For Emma

You are the energy that is truly me.
You are the power, the truth, the commitment,
The passion of life that is me.

You are always there.
Breathing for me has become your responsibility.
In your greatness you know I can breathe,
If I only, could only, would only let go.

Am I crazy? Am I losing my mind?
Sometimes those thoughts come rambling through.
Or is it just special and a blessing from you?
The loving energy that you are,
Here to be,
Expressing through me.

The feeling is sometimes overwhelming.
As you penetrate my body, my mind and my soul,
My form is on fire and then very cold.
I am relaxing and breathing and breathing some more.
The peace that comes over me is total control.

Control of nothing and everything
and just letting go.
Your laughter surrounds me,

Your humor is ever present, enlightening to all.
You have shared this for lifetimes, I know.

Slowly, slowly you continue to come.
Expressing patiently so that I will see.
My friend, my healer, is present with me,
And together we experience your presence,
Your awesomeness, your magnificent self.

We are both amazed and enchanted and
totally thrilled
At your strength and beauty unmatched
By anything either one of us has ever seen.

Your colors are vivid and bright.
Bold is your nature, and love is your song.
We feel you surround us, encompassing all.
Yellow and rose and purple you are.
The energy of color is unmistakably real.
That is how you let me know just how you feel.

Our dialogue respecting the angel you are
And knowing you will be there the next time we call.
And call you I will.

My attention is yours.
Constant the feeling of you that I have.
I will keep my body healthy and cleansed,
My mind open and patient,
And my soul loving and centered.
For your home is within me, my Spirit, my all.
September 5, 1989

Many times during the night I would be awakened by lights in my bedroom and throughout the house. This became a sign that I needed to wake up and write. And write I did! I wrote about my mother, my siblings, my son, and my childhood with my father. I cried and laughed and continued to write. At first I would tear up my writings, thinking they weren't important. As months went by, I began to save them and started to appreciate the healing that was coming as a result of this written work. More and more I became aware that I was letting go of my fears and that my heart was opening to trust. I was creating a relationship with God, and for the first time I was determined never again to feel separated from this loving connection. I was beginning to understand the power behind my thoughts, words and deeds. I had the responsibility to my self, and I could no longer deny that I was co-creating my life. By learning to respond to what life had given me, I formed a partnership with God.

I was committed to teaching my workshops wherever anyone would let me. I had no doubt that work with others was one of my life's callings. Not surprisingly, I developed workshops on learning to deal with fear and anxiety. I became passionate about my work. I felt a deep hunger for serving and giving. I wanted to teach! Doors opened everywhere for me. I enjoyed teaching in churches because I was able to speak freely of spiritual matters. This is my message: spirit-filled matters.

Between 1989-1994 I would write, study, teach, and heal. My healing has been a slow process, yet time has not been an issue. The experiences of my journey never cease to amaze me. With every step I have taken, I have felt an internal empowerment that can only be described by the word "oneness." We are all one. We are not separate from each other, yet we operate as individuals. Every thought, every word, every action we invest our energy into, affects the whole. This is the truth of the power we possess. Our grace comes when, out of love and knowing this truth, we embody the power of the One.

I will remember for the rest of my life how I felt on my fortieth birthday. On that day a veil was lifted, and I could see for the first time a future beyond anything I ever imagined. I felt born anew. I was becoming more empowered and less fearful. The anxiety that had been my constant companion was now only an occasional twinge of discomfort. Balance was the key: balance in body, emotions, mind, and spirit.

Little Bolts of Light

Even the most devastating lives have a purpose. The God spirit dwells within all of us. The key is not in understanding every event, but in how we grow spiritually because of the events.

Affirmation:

My life has a spiritual purpose.

Ten

Teaching, My Life Purpose

No matter how often I teach a workshop on learning to deal with fear, I still experience fears. As we continue to uncover our fearful selves and our old, outdated beliefs and operating systems, our fears and reactions lessen. But then new fears crop up for us, fears that require us to go even deeper into ourselves, updating our beliefs, creating newer operating systems, establishing a new comfort zone and allowing us to prepare for our next set of fears, which always come up.

The key to understanding our fears is not to be fearless, but to respond to them in an accepting, appropriate manner. This allows us to feel in control, not out of control. We are responding, not reacting. I use the word "responding" as opposed to "reacting," where we tend to lash out in order to defend ourselves.

When we respond we choose to take responsibility for our actions. We no longer need to blame others or make them or ourselves wrong. As long as we continue to grow, we will have fears. When we are asked to step into the unknown, our immediate reaction is fear. It is our natural instinct of fight or flight. I have discovered a more creative way to respond to the unknown. I now have the attitude of "I do not understand, and I do not have to." I am open and have faith that nothing can hurt me. My life is a perfect experience — for me. With faith, we have trust in the perfect outcome in all matters. The stronger our faith, the weaker our fears become.

I've had many experiences that have reinforced my desire to be open to the unknown. Some of these experiences I could not understand at the time. For example, two days before I was to teach a workshop, I had the following dream:

> *I am standing in the front lobby after church, talking to a woman about the upcoming workshop. I feel a hand tap me on my right shoulder. I turn around and face a slightly built man in a dark suit, not very tall, with a forced smile.*

> *"I need to talk to you," he says in a quiet voice, looking at me and then down at the floor.*

> *"What can I do for you?" I ask.*

> *"I really need this workshop that you*

*described this morning at the service. I heard
you speak, and every word was exactly what I
needed to hear. If I don't take this workshop, I
am going to die. I'll make sure of it. I'm
desperate and I have no money."*

*I tell him not to worry about the money,
just come the next night and we will work
something out.*

I woke up trembling. Was my success in teaching
getting to me? I decided to dismiss the dream.

The next day was Sunday, and I attended church to
give a three-minute talk on my fear workshop, which
would be held the next day. I had planned my talk
and rehearsed it well. The minister introduced me,
and as I walked to the podium my mind went blank.
I couldn't remember a thing. What was it that I had
known so well just a few moments ago?

I described my workshop, but I was not saying
what I had planned to say. I now know that what
came out of my mouth was perfect for someone in
the audience to hear. After the service I stood in the
front lobby to answer questions. I was talking to a
woman when I felt someone tap me on my right
shoulder. I turned around and faced a slightly built
man in a dark suit, not very tall, with a forced
smile. "I need to talk to you," he said in a quiet
voice, looking at me and then down at the floor —
and you know the rest. It was the man I had seen

in my dream the night before.

In 1995 I felt guided to apply to be a workshop presenter at the Native American Women's Wellness Conference, which is held annually. I wanted to call the workshop "Risking and Trusting Your Way Through Life." Although I have Yaqui Indian heritage, I was not raised with traditional native customs. I began praying for guidance. I wanted to be appropriate in my lessons and in my sharing. I wanted to love these women in the spirit of oneness. And I am sure that I desired to be accepted as one of them.

One of my fears growing up was connected to my Indian heritage. Unfortunately for me — and for those of you who understand — being Indian was considered shameful. How sad for us to have felt such an emotion! Shame is a travesty for any heritage or culture anywhere in the world. I was almost forty before I could proudly proclaim my Mexican Indian heritage. I wear it now as a badge of honor, never missing an opportunity to announce my ancestry.

My application to present the workshop was accepted. I was very excited, and yes, I was afraid. But my enthusiasm and commitment to the women were stronger than the fear and carried me through. I loved teaching that workshop, and I was asked back for the next year.

In my second year at the conference, I had a remarkable experience. I began by reading a poem by Guillaume Appollinaire:

> *Come to the edge of the cliff, he said.*
> *We are afraid, they said.*
> *Come to the edge of the cliff, he said.*
> *We are afraid, they said.*
> *Come to the edge of the cliff, he said.*
> *They came, he pushed, they flew.*

One hundred and fifty women were in the group. They were responsive, attentive, and totally present with each other and with me. I felt their spirits opening up to receiving everything I had prepared especially for them. I wanted to empower them as much as I felt empowered: the power of God, of light moving through all of us. The workshop was a great success, and after the presentation the participants lined up single file and asked for a hug. Some even wanted me to sign the handouts I had brought. I was honored and somewhat embarrassed, yet excited to be considered special to them.

One young woman waited in the front row where she had been sitting during the presentation. I had hugged everyone in line and the room was empty except for the woman who was still seated. I sat down beside her and asked what I could do for her. She took my hand and began her story: "I am from Canada. This is a far distance for me to come for a conference, but I felt a strong pull to be here. I knew there was something here that I needed to have."

She went on, "I am stuck in a situation and have not been able to move on. I am afraid. Today you talked a lot about fears and how it is all right to have them, but that we have to move on anyway so that we can discover ourselves. This I needed to hear. But the most important thing you said came right at the beginning.

Several years ago I dreamt I was standing at the edge of a cliff with a woman who said to me, 'Jump, and I will be there.' Over and over I had this dream. Each time I could not jump and would wake up crying and scared. Over and over I have thought about this dream in my waking state. I had never seen the woman in my dream before. I couldn't place her face anywhere. Finally, last week in my dream, she said again, 'Jump, and I will be with you.' We jumped together from the cliff. Our fall transformed into a soft, steady flight as we both gently landed on a beautiful, white sandy beach. I turned to look at her face and until today I did not know who she was. You are that woman whom I have seen in this dream all this time. You are the one."

She had come for her validation so that she could move on in her life. And I had come for mine, to jump and know that I too will never be alone, that I am doing the work I have prepared for: to teach, to learn, to love, and to create.

I was to facilitate a five-week workshop on "Feel the Fear and Do It Anyway," based on the book of the same title by Susan Jeffers, Ph.D. The group of over forty people would meet weekly for two hours in the evening. We began with each person introducing themselves by their first name and telling the group why they had chosen to attend the workshop.

Marge was the last one to introduce herself. She stood to tell her story. Eighteen months before, she had been involved in a serious automobile accident and hadn't driven since then. She was overwhelmed with guilt for having to ask friends for rides and could no longer stand feeling like a prisoner in her own home. She was married and not working, but she desperately needed a job. In order to work she had to drive. Her car had been totally demolished in the accident, and she had replaced it with an older car that was now parked in her carport. At this point she could not even look at the car without feeling overwhelmed by fear.

I asked everyone to stand, hold hands, and form a circle with Marge. I was comfortable asking them to pray for a healing. It was apparent that we all had been touched by her story. I asked God for strength and wisdom for Marge and for all of us gathered there. I accepted that our prayers would be answered and that we would be lifted to a higher understanding of our lives and responsibilities here on earth.

As we stood holding hands, I felt a warm flow of energy move into my right hand from the person standing next to me. This energy moved through my entire body and rushed out to the person on my left. It was an incredible feeling. This group was meeting for the first time and yet connecting at a deep level of shared love.

During our second session, Marge shared excitedly that she had sat in her car. She didn't start it up, but she sat in it. That was a beginning. Another breakthrough came the following week. This time she sat in the car and started the engine. Although she did not actually drive, she visualized driving. The group applauded her and assured her that it was only a matter of time before she would have her freedom.

In the fourth week, Marge had a setback. She couldn't even look at the car, and the thought of driving scared her more than ever. But each time we met as a group, we prayed and continued to be grateful for wisdom and strength, accepting that all is perfect in every situation and that every event is truly for our benefit.

The fifth week arrived. Marge stood to make her

announcement. "I haven't driven the car yet. I did not sit in the car this week, nor could I even look at it. Instead of driving, I have decided to file for a divorce." The group sat dumbfounded. I am sure none of us drew a breath, we were so stunned. This is not what we had expected to hear. But Marge looked better than ever. She seemed relieved and strong.

So this was it, the real fear. The imprisonment she had felt was not in her house, but in her marriage. Today Marge is single, working, driving, and feeling very grateful. The following is an excerpt from a letter she wrote to me recently:

> *Little by little, the layers started falling away and the horizons expanded. For the rest of my days I will always be thankful for having felt the fear of that first workshop. How can I feel anything but gratitude? On occasion, my lack of patience causes me to forget that I have come a very long way.*
>
> *Your friend, Marge*

I have learned to be fully present and listen without judgment to every story I am told. I know that the truth flows in everyone. Nothing is any longer unbelievable to me. Each one of us is continually given opportunities to live our lives from our essence, if we will only pay attention. Moment by moment, consciously or unconsciously, we are creating. In my most deeply centered self, I know that nothing has ever happened *to* me. It has happened *for* me. All of it has been perfect.

Little Bolts of Light

Over and over again we resist letting go of control. The truth is, we can only control our thoughts and feelings. We resist what is being prepared for us. We resist waiting for the unfoldment. We insist on trying to manipulate by fooling ourselves into believing we are actually creating something by fighting it.

Affirmation:

I release my attachment to the outcome, and I trust in the highest and best for me now.

LUZ

In 1992 I married a wonderful man who had been a client of mine for some years. Joe is an engineer. He is a kind and caring man with a quiet, thoughtful nature. I feel absolutely safe with him.

In October of 1995, I sustained an injury to my left knee during a half-marathon in San Diego. Years later the knee was so painful that I could no longer run. At Joe's insistence, I made an appointment for a check-up. He went with me to the doctor to give me emotional support. The X-rays showed a large tumor embedded inside my femur just above the knee. I was shocked and scared. The possibility of losing my leg to cancer jumped into my mind. I was sent to a bone cancer specialist. My pain worsened, and the waiting periods between visits and tests became very challenging. At the same time, I had a strong feeling of gratitude for my life. I became even more appreciative of my health and empowered state of mind.

The day before Thanksgiving I learned that the

tumor was benign and that surgery would not be necessary. But I was advised to watch for changes in the X-rays. In December I saw two other doctors and was told that my knee had to be operated on to remove the torn cartilage that was causing the pain and swelling.

I had become very sensitive to people's energies and had not yet met a doctor whom I would allow to perform the surgery. I visited very capable technicians, all highly recommended by friends and clients. But I would know immediately upon shaking hands that this person was not the one.

Around Christmastime I shared my knee story with a friend. He suggested I see a doctor friend of his. He said that the doctor was highly qualified medically and, most importantly, he described her as having healing powers — magical hands. I thanked him for the information, yet I did not want to make an appointment with this doctor. Since the tumor was benign, I decided to postpone the surgery as long as possible since the winter months in Arizona are the busiest in the beauty industry. I would wait until closer to summer to make a decision about the surgery.

On my way to work two days later, I felt my car pulling in the opposite direction of where I wanted to go. I had an impulse to follow this guidance and ended up before a building of doctors' offices. On the directory I saw the name of the doctor my friend had recommended, and my intuition told me to go directly to her office. I spoke to the receptionist and was informed that the doctor took only those patients who were referred by other doctors. I pleaded with the receptionist to give me an appointment, telling her that the doctor's personal friend had sent me. She finally consented and gave me an appointment. But she told me that they would have to cancel the appointment if the doctor would not see me.

On the morning of January 4, I was getting ready for my appointment with this doctor who had healing hands. During my shower I had a remarkable experience. As I closed my eyes to rinse my hair of shampoo, I saw a bright yellow light, so bright that it bothered my eyes to keep them closed. I blinked several times, and as I closed them again, the light became bright green and yellow with a black hole forming in the center. The hole seemed to be moving forward out of the iridescent light.

Suddenly, I felt myself being pulled through this black hole. I felt as if my entire body would fall in and be sucked through to the other side. I became scared and stretched out my hands to hold on to the walls of the shower. I called to my husband, who was in the next room, "Come quickly, there's something happening here! I feel like I'm falling into something!"

Joe is very calm and easygoing. He assured me that he would stand guard and not allow me to fall into anything or let anyone in or out, and that I would be perfectly safe in the shower until I decided to come out.

I closed my eyes for a final rinse, and the light came again. This time I felt a great sense of peace. I felt myself being asked to relax and not resist. The sound of the water turned into a low hum. I relaxed and allowed the light to warm my entire body. As the water splashed my face, I felt it gently pulling me into the black hole. I now welcomed this feeling.

The hole increased in size and depth. It was as if I were watching a movie on a huge screen. The light continued to warm my body as I traveled into the black hole, into the darkness. I moved slowly and methodically with absolutely no fear. The only words that can describe what I felt were, "I'm coming home, I'm coming home."

This experience lasted only a few minutes. I felt drained and exhilarated at the same time. I opened my eyes to find myself still in the shower and my husband standing, guarding the door, patiently clipping his fingernails. I had no clue as to what the experience meant. I did not understand, and I did not feel the need to understand.

I arrived at the doctor's office a few minutes early.

As I sat in the waiting room, a woman came in the front door. We looked at each other, smiled, and she said, "It's so good to see you again."

I smiled back and said, "It is good to see you, but I don't believe we have met?" I introduced myself. She introduced herself. She was my doctor, Marilyn. We smiled at each other as she commented, "Maybe it was in another life." She walked toward a hallway and said she would be with me in a few minutes. I liked her already.

The atmosphere of her office was informal and relaxing. Dr Marilyn came out to get me, and as we walked back toward the examining room, she apologized for her comment about knowing each other in another life. I insisted that no apology was necessary; I was perfectly comfortable with her comment. Having Emma in my life had opened me up to many possibilities that I could not logically explain.

Dr. Marilyn looked over the X-rays I had brought with me and confirmed what four other doctors had recommended: I needed surgery on the knee and I should watch for changes in the tumor. She recommended a surgeon. She also wanted to introduce me to an energy treatment called Reiki. This was a new healing method for me, but I was open to anything that would relieve the pain in my knee while I waited for surgery.

I lay face up on the examining table. The doctor rolled her stool toward my knee and gently put her hands over the swollen area to begin the Reiki treatment. She was barely touching me. I closed my eyes. Immediately the green and yellow iridescent light from that morning came back, and so did the black hole.

This time I fearlessly entered the hole, and as I did, the light turned into the marble walls of a long, narrow room. A high bed stood in the center. On the far wall a small window opened to a blue-green sky. The room seemed sterile and cold. Two women were there. One was lying on the bed in hard labor, and the other was assisting in the delivery. This was a birthing room. I was the woman in labor! I could see the ceiling through tears which flooded my eyes, and I could feel the pain of labor in my lower back. It was almost over. I felt myself sweating, tears streaming down the sides of my face. I pushed and moaned. In my final push, I looked up at the woman helping me with the delivery. It was Marilyn, my doctor.

I gave birth to a girl. Marilyn placed the baby on my naked belly for a few moments so that I could hold her. Then she took the baby in her arms, walked to the open window, and held her up to show her to whoever was outside. I heard drums and bells and people cheering as they saw my baby girl. A celebration was going on outside the window! Although I could not see the people, I could hear their excitement. Another woman entered the room. Marilyn handed the baby to her. She wrapped my daughter in a white blanket and left the room with her. Starting with my feet, Marilyn slowly washed my entire naked body. The water was warm and soothing. She finished by washing my hair. I remember lots of water, lots of rinsing, and then more water.

I awoke from this dream and opened my eyes. Marilyn had moved up from my knee and was looking in my face. I lay there exhausted, sweating, tears streaming down my face.

"In what other life do you think we knew each other?" I asked.

She had the most beautiful, gentle face I had ever looked into. In her soft voice she answered, "Maybe the Pleiades. I think maybe there."

I pretended to know what she was talking about. I had no clue what the Pleiades were. I was too exhausted and shocked by this incredible experience to respond.

I stood up. My legs were weak. We hugged for a moment, but I didn't want to let her go. She felt so familiar. As she held me she said, "I've been told that you're going to be just fine. All is well."

I made an appointment for another visit, and

before I left, she asked me for my business card. She said she would call me for an appointment to have her hair done.

On my way out the door I heard her words again: "I've been told you're going to be just fine. All is well." Who had told her? Who was talking to her? Where would my life take me next? The biggest question I had was about the shower incident. The colors and the black hole had all preceded my visit to Marilyn. How could I or some part of me have known the experience I was going to have two hours later in her office?

It was difficult going to work that day; I would rather have gone home to bed. My mind kept trying to make sense of what had happened, and my feelings kept trying to enjoy the whole experience. I couldn't wait to see my husband that evening. Joe is well read and always seems to know something about everything.

We met at a little restaurant for dinner. Joe was already seated at the table when I arrived. I sat down and asked him, "What are the Pleiades?"

Joe explained, "They are a star system. Astronomers estimate that they are about 100 million years old. The ancient Egyptians and Greeks studied them and wrote about them. In mythology they were called the 'Seven Sisters,' after the seven daughters of the Greek god, Atlas.

About three hundred years ago, one of the seven stars seems to have disappeared. It had apparently collapsed into itself and left only six sisters, six visible stars. Some astronomers think that the star is still there, just not visible. They really aren't sure."

"What could have happened to the one sister who disappeared?" I asked.

"They believe it may have turned into a black hole," he answered.

This took my breath away. I told him about my day, beginning with the shower experience, falling into a black hole, then meeting Marilyn, who suggested that we had met in the Pleiades. We went over the day several times. I knew that I did not have to understand it right now. Answers would evolve as they all eventually do.

Two weeks later, Marilyn came for her hair appointment. I usually work with an assistant who shampoos my clients. This day my assistant was unavailable, so I shampooed Marilyn's hair myself. As I bent over her to rinse out the shampoo, we looked at each other and simultaneously said, "It's good to be with you again." We both felt a connection that went beyond the words we spoke, beyond this lifetime, beyond what we understood.

We have continued our professional relationship.

Marilyn became my doctor, and I became her hair-dresser. We have also developed a lasting personal relationship that goes beyond friendship. We share a unique bond and accept simply that we love and cherish each other. She blessed me immensely by assisting the doctor when I finally had my knee surgery. Imagine how safe, loved and supported I felt that day, having her there. I was feeling even more inner power, the power that only comes through the awareness of the self and our mental, emotional, and spiritual oneness with everything.

As for the green and yellow light I met in the shower that day — its name is Luz, which is Spanish for "light." Luz has been with me ever since. Just as my angel has remained my steady companion, so has Luz. I see Luz mostly in my morning shower. It communicates with me by its light. When the light is bright, I am going to experience something special that day. It could be a person or situation that will raise my consciousness to a higher level. If the light is not bright but is still there, it's just a signal of connecting with me. We have developed a dialogue between us that works. Luz is a beacon, a sign for me to become expectantly aware of something I am about to experience.

As afraid as I was the fist time I met Luz, I now welcome my "light." Sometimes it leaves for a week or so, but it always comes back. Two years ago it came to me on my birthday while I was making breakfast in the kitchen. At first I was stunned. I wasn't expecting it. But here was Luz, wishing me happy birthday. If you are wondering how I know this and how I came to know its name, it told me. It told me without speaking a word. I just felt it. Luz and I communicate through my feelings.

The story of Luz may sound hard to believe, and if someone had shared it with me ten years ago, I would have run the other way. I don't ask anyone to believe the story, nor do I share it often. But Luz is my messenger, my guide, my companion from the other side of this world. I do not know how to explain it any other way. I do not understand it beyond what I am sharing now. It is what it is — my connection to unlimited possibilities. It is my connection to more of the untapped, mystical universe.

I see Luz often, along with Emma, who I feel alongside me as I write this book. Who are they? Do all of us have angels and guides? I say, "Ask and you shall receive. Accept and you will be blessed beyond your dreams."

Little Bolts of Light

God has a way of coming into our lives through experiences that we resist believing. Dr. Wayne Dyer said it best: "You'll see it when you believe it."

Affirmation:

**God has already given me everything.
I only need to become conscious of this.**

Twelve

↑

My Ministry

When Dr. Reed insisted that I reintroduce myself to God for my physical healing, he could not have imagined how much I would embrace God. Nor could I have ever believed how accepting God would affect my future. I wanted to develop a relationship with a loving Creator, and I also wanted to develop within myself the security and safety that I had tried desperately to find in other people.

Through my traditional Catholic background I had developed a fear of being punished and judged by a heavenly father. My fear of a father-imaged God had permeated all of my male relationships. My relationships with men had been very unhealthy because of this. Until I finally understood where the belief and fear came from, they controlled my life. When I made the decision to heal my relationship with God, my human relationships began to heal spiritually and emotionally.

I decided to study in depth the Science of Mind teachings. My fellow students and I shared the same pains and the desire to connect with a loving God. All of us were looking for our spiritual home. During this time I developed a faith in God that words cannot express. I am unable to describe the moments of bliss and gratitude that are deeply buried in my soul as a result of our studies together. Silently, I would sit for hours and feel myself being loved by this deep connection that I could not interpret. I welcomed time for reading, writing, and meditating as often as I could. I spent much time alone, no longer afraid of my own thoughts.

My passion became sharing with others what I had learned about spiritual principles. My ministry began with no horns tooting or banners flowing. It began as I stood at my station in my beauty salon and saw change occur as I talked my clients through their problems. They became beautiful outside and inside at the same time.

I had learned how to help others because I was no longer afraid of myself and my thoughts. I had learned the secret to answered prayer. "Seek Ye First the Kingdom of God and All Else Shall Be Added."

Life was good. My work at the salon and my outside speaking and teaching engagements flourished. I developed a strong sense of security and faith in myself. This feeling came in learning that the universe is always on purpose, always in perfect order. Nothing haphazard ever happens. Every event gives us the opportunity to either connect with the Source or to separate. The choice is mine. The more I realized that safety comes from my inner connection with God, the safer I felt. Nothing on the outside could take anything away from me.

My faith strengthened as I honored the Oneness of all things. No matter what I did, I would always be connected. Nothing could ever separate me from God again. When God is missing from my life, I am the one who chooses to leave.

The Science of Mind studies were to take five years. After four years, I felt confident that I had learned enough, so I dropped out of class before completing the last year of my practitioner training. I told myself that the tools and information I had acquired during those years were all that I needed. I was feeling spiritually, emotionally, and physically strong. My fellow students at the Church of Religious Science started their last year of practitioner training without me.

I began taking classes in communications and psychology at the local junior college. But within two months I felt out of balance. Something was missing in my life. There were no challenges that I couldn't handle, but I felt anxious. What had happened to those feelings of safety and faith?

It had been four years since I'd had a panic attack. I knew the subtle signs and could feel them creeping back. As much as I prayed and meditated, the feelings would not go away. I felt my connection with God had been severed. Home alone one evening, getting ready for my college class, I experienced a paralyzing panic attack. God! How I dreaded the pain that accompanied this confusion and isolation. All of my fears came flooding back to me. But this time I would not cave in to them.

I immediately began the process of caring for myself. I went back to see Dr. Reed. He said, "Begin acupuncture treatment, food testing, and counseling. And let go of college classes." He left out one thing: Close the split that separated me from God and heal it. And guess what that was?

I applied to re-join my practitioner class in Science of Mind. I asked if I might be allowed to make up the three months I had missed. I had been a good student, and I knew I was a capable and responsible person. A week later I was welcomed back in. It felt good to be in this loving, spiritual atmosphere once more.

I completed my practitioner training with my classmates and took the written test. Two weeks later I received a phone call with the news that I had not passed the examination. I had missed passing by five points. For a moment there was only silence. Time stopped.

I heard the voice on the line say, "Are you O.K.?"

I answered, "Yes, I'm fine."

"What are you feeling?"

" I feel relieved."

I honestly didn't know why I had such a feeling. No matter how I tried, I could not explain my feeling of relief.

One week later I became angry! First I called the minister in charge of practitioner training and asked if I had any recourse. Could I take the examination again? She explained that I could take the examination again in one year. I called the Religious Science main office and asked if I could appeal the decision, but I was told that the rule was to wait a year and then take it again. I couldn't change the rules!

Gradually, my anger began to disappear. I began to let go of trying to control or change what had happened. I couldn't fix it. I remembered that everything happens in divine order. There are no accidents in the universe. As I had learned in my spiritual studies, the universe is always on purpose! I had finished my work, and now I would simply wait until the next door opened. I felt secure in my decision to do nothing.

Three years later, during a very busy day in my salon, I received a call from my friend and former therapist. She and her husband were considering bringing a spiritual counselor to their thriving practice and wanted me to take the position. I was surprised and delighted.

But I said, "Don't you remember? I didn't pass my examination. I'm not a licensed practitioner."

"How long will it take you to get that license?" she asked.

I answered, "I don't know what I can do at this point. I'll check on it and call you back." I thanked her for her generous offer and hung up the phone.

I hadn't thought about a license or the ministry in several years. After I hung up, I couldn't stop thinking of the possibilities. Not necessarily to take the offer from my therapist and her husband, but to resume my goal of sharing spiritual wisdom with others in an official capacity.

I was standing in the salon, wrapping a perm. Other clients were waiting in various stages of their hair process. My thoughts flashed back to Reverend Linda, the woman who tutored me during my Science of Mind studies. She had taken her ministerial training at a local metaphysical seminary. Within ten minutes we were talking. Yes, she knew of a woman in Mesa, Arizona, who could help me. Dr. Mary Alice Edgerton had been the director of the New Thought Seminary in

Mesa. She had retired two years earlier but was still around. She could probably guide me to someone who could help.

I began to feel a warming sensation all over my body. I had been teaching the principles through my workshops and classes for several years. No one had ever questioned my credentials. Up came the old longing for the status that I felt only a license from an accredited seminary could provide. It just happened that Reverend Linda was meeting Dr. Edgerton Sunday for church and lunch afterwards. Would I like to join them?

At lunch I shared my desire to become a licensed spiritual teacher and told of my history of spiritual studies and my experience in presenting workshops. This pleased and excited Dr. Edgerton.

"I'm sorry that I'm retired," she said, "because I would love to work with you."

Reverend Linda didn't miss an opportunity and quickly asked, "Why don't you?"

I jumped in and asked, "What would it take to have you help me?"

"I suppose I could put together a class for you. We would have to become accredited through a spiritual institution, form an educational arm, and find several students to study with you. Also, I suggest you go for your ministerial certification, which includes becoming a spiritual counselor."

Within a month I was enrolled in ministerial school. Dr. Edgerton, who I now called Mary Alice, came out of retirement and formed Seminary Services Network, an educational program created for the purpose of accrediting people desiring to complete their ministerial training. She took me on what she called a "fast track," and that it was. Our group met twice a week. Five of us studied together. I read twenty books, studied the New Testament, and wrote a thesis on how I discovered and used truth. I wrote marriage, memorial, and christening ceremonies and many "treatments" for practitioner review.

My year of study came to a close. There was one more bridge to cross before my ordination, and that was the oral board interview with five independent Religious Science ministers. Everyone was relaxed and having fun but me! I just wanted them to get on with it! When the two-hour interview was over, I waited in the church sanctuary for the outcome. Dr. Mary Alice had assured me that I was so prepared that I would pass with flying colors. When the door opened and I was called in for the board decision, I saw five smiling faces and some tears, too. Thank you, Mother-Father-God.

Over one hundred friends and family members came to celebrate my ordination into the ministry.

My mother and father were there and cried the tears of proud parents. My brother and sisters with their families sat together. My sister Maggie, along with two other friends, greeted guests as they arrived. I felt great love for my family, and secretly, as I looked out at them, I thought of what it had been like for us growing up. Who would have ever imagined one of us would become a minister?

As I walked down the aisle and up to the podium to join Dr. Mary Alice, my husband and son followed. My heart was full as I looked out at the audience. I saw the faces of people who knew my life story intimately. I felt their love, and the support they held for me was vibrantly alive.

I turned to face my son. From the day that he was born, I have not loved anyone as deeply as I love him. Tragedies and miracles have come my way, but nothing has occupied my thoughts as much as he. I looked at him as he placed my ministerial robe around my shoulders. Bending down to kiss me, his eyes filled with tears. At twenty-five, he was lean and boyish, and yet so grown up. I had everything. Every day that I had ever lived had brought me here to this moment, right now. I felt one with God, one with my husband and son, and with every person there. There could be no separation from anything or anyone. All I felt on this day was total faith, love, and pure joy.

My son Ron and I collaborated in writing this poem, which was read at the ordination:

The Train

I'm riding on a train.
I know not its destination, nor does it seem to
matter.
I hear a voice calling in the distance,
"Come along, my friends, and those I've yet
to meet,
Come along and join me and do not be
afraid."

Mighty is the Spirit of this train on which I ride,
Mystical its nature.
"Come along and play this game of wonder,
And do not be afraid."

The train travels through many stations.
At each stop the message is the same,
"Come along and play this game of wonder,
And do not be afraid."

The train of life I call it,
Stopping and starting only for a while,
Picking up and dropping off.
Gently, slowly, moving right along,
Not knowing where my destination.
No matter, for I am not alone.

What drives this vehicle in motion?
What power gives it strength?

Closer and closer to the front I go.
I am looking for the Source on which it runs,
Anticipating burning coal
or any other energy on which to draw.
Then suddenly, but only for a moment,
I am sure I know.
The truth from which the power comes
Is deep inside of me.

I am the power, the energy that moves
my train.
I am the power, the energy. I am the train.

Since my ordination I have become a spiritual counselor part-time. My life is diverse and interesting. I am still a hairdresser and work-shop presenter, and I also bring together women and men with vision to network with each other and hear inspiring speakers. As I live on the other side of fear and create my life through what I love to do, it unfolds beautifully in ways that I could not have imagined.

Little Bolts of Light

It is never too late. When we finally understand that we are one with God, no matter what age or what space we are occupying, that is the perfect time for all possibilities.

Affirmation:

I always have enough time to do what I love.

Thirteen

Give Us This Day
Our Daily Bread

For those of you who are able to eat bread, either home-baked fresh from the oven or from the bakery in a variety of choices, I say enjoy it! I am allergic to wheat, so it has been many years since I have tasted this delicious food. The subject I want to address here is not bread itself, but eating as a conscious choice.

My body has been one of my greatest teachers. Even as a child, food was an indicator of things that needed my attention. I do not remember at what age this began. If my memory serves me, it was in the seventh grade. My abdomen would swell after each meal, and at times I had a hard time breathing. After lunch I would often put my head down on my desk and try to relax so that I could breathe. Inevitably I would be reprimanded for not paying attention. Afraid to say anything and ashamed to appear stupid, I never said anything about this to anyone.

My stomach and eating problems continued into

my adult years. As I mentioned earlier, in my early twenties I began starving myself to death. After dozens of tests and many visits to specialists, I was diagnosed with Hystericus, better known as Globus Hysteria. I know now that this condition was a result of emotional trauma. I also know that women suffer with more stomach and eating-related problems than men. Not only is it what we are eating, it's what's eating us.

My pain was not just in my mind, it was in all of me. Then I did not know that the body's wellbeing is connected to our emotional and spiritual wellbeing. I was given medication to stop the pain in my stomach, but few doctors knew enough to go beyond traditional western medicine to help me discover the cause of the pain. The Valium I took only masked my problems. I wanted someone to show me the pathway to health or at least help me understand my disease and my responsibility with it. What I needed was a holistic approach to health.

Many factors are involved in health issues, but I am sure that eating well is imperative for healing. We are the most weight-conscious society in the world, yet statistics show that over half of our country's population is obese. Why is this? A third of our population is on medication for emotional problems. What is the relationship, if any, between emotional problems and eating?

My food allergies, food sensitivities, and other

food-related problems and dysfunctions have motivated me to set a standard of eating that has not only given me energy but also created an honoring relationship between me and my body. The bottom line is that I have been gifted in having to eat a very healthy diet.

The most questionable foods we take into our systems are sugar, wheat, yeast, dairy, preservatives, MSG, highly processed foods, and all those chemicals whose names I cannot pronounce or spell. In the past when I would eat these foods I would go into anaphylactic shock, which caused me to stop breathing.

With the help of my nutritionist, Kathleen Hosner, I have succeeded in fine-tuning my regime into a joyful experience of eating. As for bread, which I cannot eat, I have this great substitute that looks like bread and meets my desire for an occasional sandwich!

My eating regime is simple: I eat as natural and uncomplicated foods as possible. My diet consists primarily of vegetables, protein, fruits, nuts, goat cheese, beans, and grains. I eat organic foods whenever possible. Sometimes this requires that I take food with me when I am traveling or away from home. I eat small portions of food about six times a day. I pay attention to how I combine certain foods; for instance, I eat fruits by themselves. I drink cold water in between meals, with or without lemon, and I drink no liquids with meals. I enjoy a glass of juice daily. My favorite is fresh-squeezed orange juice. This is my diet, and it works for me. Occasionally, I have a chocolate chip cookie or lightly salted organic chips with delicious Mexican salsa. I savor every bite of these special treats!

Personally, I do take supplements that have been prescribed by a nutritionist but have learned not to push supplements, vitamins, or any other diet regime on anyone else. Each body has its own holographic patterns that must be honored. It is important to get professional assistance in determining the diet that is right for you. More and more professionals in holistic practice are including a thoughtful diet and exercise as essential to a person's wellbeing.

I believe that what I eat affects not only my body, but the body of humanity. We are all connected, sharing our lives in spiritual, universal relationship. My friend and nutritional consultant, Kathleen, says it best this way: "What we eat directly affects the planetary ecology and the degree of peace we have with ourselves and with the human, animal, and plant life on the planet. Our diet and the way we live our lives directly reflects our inner harmony with the Divine."

I encourage you to take full responsibility and not give up to a world that makes changes to the body by removing or changing its parts. We stretch our bodies, have parts made bigger or smaller, suck parts out and have others lifted. We spend billions of dollars every year working on the outside of our bodies, taking dangerous risks, and we neglect our inner emotional and spiritual needs.

Often I hear people say, "Why so much attention to the body? We are spiritual beings having a human experience."

I say, "I agree."

And where is this spirit being housed? It's not in a tree or a rock. They have their own spirits. Ours is in our bodies.

I share this information with you because it has been a vital part of my healing journey. Eating well has helped save my life and has given me the energy and vitality to pursue life with purpose, passionately. I am serious about my body and my commitment to love and respect such a beautiful, living organism.

Little Bolts of Light

Deny your body and you deny God!

Affirmation:

**I honor my body
as my spiritual vessel.**

Fourteen

And God Created Hairdressers

9 began my career as a hairdresser at the age of eight. Playing with my Barbie doll, I would style her hair into updo's, braids, pageboys, and pony tails. Not thinking that her hair would not grow back, I created my first short style, the Bubble. This ended our relationship. She never booked another appointment!

From Barbie I moved on to real people. During my high school years I developed a clientele of neighbors and friends who actually paid me to cut and style their hair. I transformed my bedroom into a salon. Saturday mornings were busy with hair brushes, rollers, and hair spray. I used stale beer for setting lotion. The blow dryer and curling iron had not reached my hometown, so the existence of such tools was beyond my imagination.

Entering cosmetology school was a natural for me when I left home and moved to Phoenix. While my high school classmates enrolled in college for four years of studies and eventual degrees, I could complete my schooling in nine months and have a license to begin my career. I envied my classmates and wished I had the same opportunity, but my grades were not strong enough, and my parents could not afford such a luxury. My priority, as I have mentioned, was to become self-sufficient as soon as possible.

I clearly remember my goal as I completed my schooling: I would work for only a few years, meet Mr. Perfect, get married, have children, and stay home. Hairdressing was simply a way to make money.

Over thirty years have passed since I began this journey of helping people feel good about themselves through cosmetology. I have met thousands of people, both men and women, who have been my clients. Through this career I have been given great blessings, rewards, friendships, financial successes, and learning experiences. In my wildest dreams as a young woman beginning beauty school, I could never have imagined a life so alive and fulfilling.

Before I began my spiritual path, touching people with my hands and doing their hair or make up was only a service I provided. As I became more aware of the energy fields of our bodies, both physical and etheric, I realized the depth of connection that goes on between two people in the dance of exchanging these energies. No less than a cosmic event occurs when, with conscious choice, a person decides to enter into a relationship of touching another person. My friend, Dr. Howard Silverman, was the first person to express this openly and specifically to me as a first-time client. I asked him, as I ask all new clients, "What is it that I can do for you?" The essence of his reply was, "I want to be touched by someone who is conscious." I remember feeling strange because I actually understood him, and I was honored that he would think this about me.

I know that our learning process as humans is to have experiences and to repeat behaviors until a lesson is learned, but I do not always like it. If I had one thing to do over, it would be to have appreciated the sacred dynamics of cosmetology from the beginning. I would like to meet again every client that sat in my chair. When I was entrenched in my own pain and learning experiences with fear, anger, and doubt, each client must have felt it at some level. I can only say this: Give me another chance in the next life. I have faith that I will be wiser.

From the beginning of time, beautifying one another has been an important part of cultural tradition and ritual. Ancient historical record keepers and artists carved and painted scenes of men and women being dressed, pampered, and coiffed in preparation for rituals and ceremonies. The Greeks and Egyptians paid much attention to the meaning of luxury and nurturing the body by beautifying themselves with elaborate baths, oils, massage, wigs, and makeup.

One of the most profound experiences I have led women through in workshop retreats is an exercise that demonstrates the deep feelings that come with unconditional giving and receiving. The exercise is hair brushing. Gathered in a candle-lit room with soft and soothing music, as many as sixty women at a time have shared this affectionate, touching ritual. Half the women sit in chairs. The other half stand behind them and from their hands and hearts give an unconditional gift, the gift of brushing the hair. The women who are sitting are asked to think only of the feelings that come from receiving this unconditional gift. As the music plays, the women relax deeply. Tears escape from their eyes, as they are flooded with feelings and memories that only they can know.

There is an honoring that is intrinsic in the beautifying of someone else. A sisterhood is developed between two women who share their intimate stories. My closest relationships, including my husband and dearest friends, have been born through the men and women who have been my clients.

Cherished comments and moments will be with me until the day I die. One client, whom I see every three weeks, said as I was trimming his beard, mustache, and eyebrows: "I've been married all my life, and do you know that you touch me more than my wife does?" This was a sad statement, yet not unusual to hear in my chair. In a world where rape, sexual harassment, and sex addicts get the attention, I believe that most people are starving just to be touched in an honoring and respectful way. There is something very relaxing about having your head massaged and your hair combed and played with. We hairstylists know that the roles of confessor, advisor, and listener are a very important part of our work.

Another important activity goes on during this energetic exchange — the stimulation of the seventh chakra. This energy center is located at the top of the head. It is one of seven power centers of a complex "database" that houses the energetic system that controls our physical, emotional, mental, and spiritual bodies. In her book *Energy Anatomy*, Caroline Myss, Ph.D., says: "This is the entry point for the human life force, which pours endlessly into the human energy system from the greater universe, from God or the Tao. It contains the energy that generates devotion, inspiration, and prophetic thoughts, transcendent ideas and mystical connections. This is the center of Oneness."

Two other chakras are also on or near the head: the sixth, which is located at the center of the forehead, and the fifth, which is located at the throat. The sixth represents the mind and clarity; the fifth represents our will. I experience the energy of all three chakras in my work with clients. Once I stood behind a client, running my fingers from her temples over the top of her head and down the back of it to the nape of her neck as I prepared to section her hair for a cut. I experienced electrical pulses running through my hands into my arms and into my chest, which literally took my breath away. I felt as though we were breathing with the same lungs and moving the same blood through our bodies.

I do not usually discuss these sensations with my clients, nor do I tell them when I see color in and around their bodies. There is one experience, though, that I would like to share with you. I had one client who was in his early thirties, committed to a successful career, and, I thought, extremely handsome. I enjoyed talking with him during his haircut appointments, but there was something about him that made me uncomfortable. I assumed that his handsome appearance was the cause of my discomfort, so I let it go at that.

One day he called for a quick trim, and the receptionist had not yet informed me that he was due to come in. While I was working on a client, I heard the door open and looked up. I could not make out the person walking toward me. All I could see was bright, hot, brilliant red. As the person came closer, I could feel anger, and I sensed that it was deep and long-suffering. In my mind's eye, I saw a young boy being reprimanded by his father. The boy's face showed no emotion, but his hands were clenched and his throat was tight, holding back the urge to scream. As the person came closer, I recognized the face of the handsome man and also understood my previous discomfort. I had felt his anger before. Later, while we were alone and I was trimming his hair, I asked him about his childhood. He told me about it openly and honestly. He had been abused and shamed by his father all his life. Before coming to his appointment, he had talked with his mother and had made plans to visit his parents. The anger that still ran deep in his heart had been stirred up, and he carried it into the salon with him.

I could tell story after story of experiences that do not have a rational explanation. The truth is, something mystical is happening all around us. Most of us are too afraid to allow ourselves to explore beyond the physical boundaries of our lives. But where the intention is to raise our consciousness, in helping people feel better about themselves and understand themselves more clearly, anything is possible.

I will be eternally grateful to the beauty industry, which has been so good to me. I know that God directed me and led me to this career.

Pressures and demands are also, of course, part of this work. Recently, a client came in complaining loudly about my schedule. She was quite upset and told me that I should work more hours to accommodate her schedule. She demanded special attention. I styled her hair, and afterward, we looked over my books and made several appointments that accommodated both our schedules. As she walked out the door, my niece, Veronica, who works as my assistant, looked at me with frustration and said, "Aunt Hilda, doesn't that woman know who you are?"

"Yes," I replied. "I'm her hairdresser!"

Little Bolts of Light

No matter where you are, you are creating and manifesting your blessings.

Affirmation:

I am in my perfect place for manifesting my blessings.

Fifteen

The Search
for My Roots

During the years I spent in therapy, the most difficult, yet the most life-changing and empowering work that I did concerned my relationship with my father. Over and over I revisited my memories of terror that resulted in my low self-esteem, anger, anxiety, and obsessive neurotic behavior. This exploration was not an easy journey, but one that I was totally committed to.

I knew so little about my father's own childhood, not because I didn't ask him, but because he gave very little information about himself. His answer was always the same: "I don't remember much." He said almost nothing about his own father. Most of the information I learned from my mother.

My father, Dionicio, was born in Mesa, Arizona in 1926. His mother Romana, a Yaqui Indian, had come to the States from Mexico to work in the melon fields. She was a widow with three young children, and she was pregnant with her fourth child. This work was the only way she knew to provide for her children. In Mesa she met Cliofas, also of Mexican-Indian heritage, who had come to Arizona to work for the railroad. They became the parents of my father.

My mother, Maria Parra, was born in Tubutama, Sonora, Mexico. Both her parents were of Spanish ancestry. Her father, Jose, was tall, light-skinned, and light-eyed. He was a handsome man, a blacksmith by profession. Her mother, Magdalena, whom my sister Maggie is named after, died in childbirth along with her baby, when my mom was only three years old. Mom was raised by relatives and her father, who moved often. Most of her childhood was spent raising stepbrothers and sisters and other children. She was handed from one family to the next.

At the age of six, when his parents moved from Arizona to Sonora, Mexico, Dad started his first job. He and his older cousin, Enriquita, who was eight, joined a band. My dad played the drums. The band performed in downtown Santa Ana at bars and at any gathering that would have them. Dad worked four days a week and went to school when he could. By the time he was eight he had taught himself to play other instruments, and he was hired by a group called "El Trio." With them he earned two dollars a week.

At the age of twelve, he dropped out of school completely and went to work full-time as a musician in a house of prostitution. Here he would spend the next seven years until, at the age of nineteen, he moved back to Arizona and worked as a laborer in the copper mine. He worked in the mine for almost forty years.

In therapy, I had to put myself in my father's place. What did he know? How did he come to view women, and what experiences might he have had with women? What pain was he trying to suppress with alcohol? Why might he have treated us the way he did? Could I at least try to understand his behavior?

More than ten years have passed since I first began therapy. It has been a slow process for me, but I have learned to understand my father and to unconditionally love and forgive him. The more I am able to love him, the more I am able to love myself. The more I love myself, the more I am able to love others. The less fearful I am of being hurt, the more I can love him for his role in making possible the determined and loving personality that I have been able to create for myself.

Recently I visited my father and told him that I was writing this book. It was a painful conversation, but through it an important dialogue opened up between us. Never before had he shared with me his own violent and abusive childhood. He told me that when he was a boy, his father would severely beat his wife, Romana, my grandmother, and then turn to him and beat him nearly to death because he tried to come to the aid of his mother. His parents separated for months at a time, but eventually they would reunite for more of the same. My father told me that the reason he worked at such a young age was to support his mother in the hopes that she would leave his father for good.

Many people have experienced similar pain, fear, and love of their parents. It is important to know that we are not alone, that we are here to learn to love and to create our lives through love. As painful as my father's story is, I share it with you because I am continuously impressed by the resiliency of the human spirit.

During our last visit my father said to me, "I tried my best to be a good father to you and your brother and sisters. I tried my best."

I looked at him, took him in my arms, and held him tightly for a few moments. "I know you did, Dad. I'm sure you did." I telephone my father twice a month. He lives in a tiny town in southern Arizona, just thirty minutes from Mexico. He owns a two-room home in the middle of the desert. His life is simple and he requires very little to exist.

I am not making excuses for my father's behavior. I don't have to. What happened is in the past. Every day, every minute, I make choices. I can choose anger, resentment, or vindication. I can also choose peace, acceptance, and love.

I love my father. I choose to. He is the only father I will know in this lifetime. I provide plenty of boundaries for myself and spend very little time with him. He hasn't changed much except that he is alone, very alone. His entire life revolves around the television schedule and reading the Holy Bible.

My parents were married thirty-two years before Mom finally filed for divorce. Two years later my father married a woman from Mexico who had worked as a prostitute to support her children. They were married for twelve years until she passed away from cancer. She tolerated his insistent, demanding nature and cared for him until the day she died.

Mom remarried also. She chose a man who is an alcoholic. Ed had been a friend of the family for over twenty years and had often rescued us during our hard times with Dad. I am sure Mom appreciated his support. Ed had been there to give us all a helping hand. I am grateful for his generosity to us.

Yes, my mother married more of the same. She suffers no physical abuse, but I think the verbal abuse is just as painful. They don't have much, but what they do have gives her a feeling of security, something she never had with our father. Ed is now fading away with cirrhosis of the liver and diabetes. Mom and I talk every day by phone, and we are very close. There is a saying in Mexico: *Hijos de la mala vida*. It translates: "Children of the bad life." Mom used to say this often, herself a victim of the bad life.

I have begun to introduce her to new spiritual ideas. She has started reading the *Daily Word* and other books that can empower her and give her hope. Slowly they have begun to make sense to her. At times I see her peaceful and relaxed, although much of the time she seems tired and worried.

As I witness her aging, I want to give her some moments of fun, something she has rarely experienced. She loves the airplane, and I look forward to taking her on another trip. I will never forget the look of excitement on her face when I took her on her first plane ride a couple of years ago!

I love my mother and cannot change her life from what she expects it to be. She is a loving and devoted mother to her children, grandchildren, and great-grandchildren. My mother, more than any other woman, taught me how to love. She has loved me no matter what I did, said, or didn't do. Her love for me is unconditional, as is her love for the rest of her children. Yes, the universe knew what it was doing when it gave me my mother, Maria.

Little Bolts of Light

Our parents: they did what they had to with the circumstances of their lives.

Affirmation:

**I accept the foundation
of my life as the perfect place to
have come from.**

Sixteen

Fear, the Beloved Adversary

$\mathcal{A}$s children, no matter our circumstances, life happens *for us*, not *to us*. During our earliest years we gather information and establish belief systems based on our experiences. We take these belief systems into our adult lives. They become the basis of discovering and developing our true essence. There are many ways we come to know our essence. Most of us choose the path of discovery through resistance, doubt, and separateness. All of these ways stem from fear. In order to transform fear, we must accept it as a natural and vital emotion that guides us toward our true essence. The journey to this essence is what we call our life purpose.

Fear assists our growth because it always imposes limitations on us. Our job is to empower ourselves by moving beyond these limitations. Our challenge comes in the choice to commit to the journey of discovering and changing our self-imposed limitations. First, we become aware of our beliefs and how we learned them. Second, we choose to change these beliefs and develop new, healthier, supportive ones. Third, we commit to a lifetime of living our true essence, which always expresses itself through some aspect of love.

Great power lies within all of us. This is not a supernatural or extraordinary power. In fact, it is the truth of who we were born to be. "God created man in His own image, in the image of God He created Him, male and female He created them." (Genesis 2-27) The key word here is *created*. We were born to create, to explore, to advance.

Fear is our primary emotion for survival. It can save us or we can be ruined by it. When we stay afraid, we are uncertain. This emotion is important in the creative process. Fear and uncertainty become conduits for creativity and innovation. We perceive fear as our enemy, and yet confronting our relationship with fear can force us into our most imaginative and productive thinking. We do not want to throw away the fear and never feel it. We want to use it for awakening and growth. Fear is indeed the beloved adversary.

Only one other emotion motivates me more than fear, and that is love. At times I have found it difficult to differentiate if it was fear or love that I was feeling. Being too afraid to love, I would act on my fears.

I was intrigued recently by a Science of Mind article in which I read the following excerpt:

How to Get Something and Keep It

There are two ways to get something and keep it: love it or fear it. This is because the subconscious knows only the intensity of our desires or fears. It can't distinguish beyond that, or it would be in there interfering with our choices. (Stop! You don't want that!) Of course, nobody deliberately chooses to have more of what they fear. Instead, they don't realize that by fearing it, they're expanding it. Both love and fear generate cycles of creativity, where more of the same keeps arriving. To have more of what we want, rather than what we don't want, we must move our emotions off the picture of what we don't want. Emotion flows where we direct it.

When we become afraid, what is truly going on? What is it that we need to pay close attention to? How many times has fear forced us to make a decision to move on, to stay, to call our spirit back, to take a stand, or to cry for help? How many times has fear pulled us into action in a situation which in the past had paralyzed us? Can you see how fear has supported you in transforming your own life?

We must consider: Did I create this? Is there a

Creator who created it for me? Or are we one and the same? Every creation we manifest moves us closer to the consciousness of the One.

I now think back on the hours, weeks, months, and years I spent afraid of what might happen and trying to change things. Searching for a solution on how to stop this barrage of mind chatter, I never looked inside myself for the answer. *Think of what you love, and create that.* How different would my life have been had I done this earlier? How much easier it is for me now that I use this information. And yet I am sure that I needed to live in uncertainty so that I could have created all that I have in my life. I would not change one single moment, and I would do it all over again.

I am convinced that my entire life had been a continual feeding of the hunger I developed as a child, the hunger to feel safe and secure. I searched for safety and security outside myself. My fear would starve me almost to death as I insisted that someone outside me should feed me and stop my hunger. This search became my greatest blessing.

Until we realize that fear is only present to help us get to a spiritual awakening of the Truth, we continue to perceive fear as bad. Imagine your thoughts shifting from *I am afraid, and I do not understand* to: *I allow the emotion of fear and release it to the spiritual me that understands.* Whatever I hold in my consciousness I will create. Today I choose to hold on to love. Fear or love: it is completely up to me.

I believe that there is only one real purpose for all of us, and that is to become spiritually conscious. Using affirmations, praying with a grateful heart, meditating, listening, eating consciously, mindful walking, and any other spiritual practice you choose becomes your discipline and your commitment to this process.

My friend Marilyn Powers taught me the value of affirmative statements during my years of therapy with her. Because they are so valuable, I have included affirmations at the end of each chapter. In addition to these, I would like to share some other affirmations that have supported me:

> **When dealing with doubt:** *"Something greater than me is in control of this situation. I surrender to the Divine plan for me now. I claim a greater good upon me now. My faith is limitless and has no end."*

> **When feeling separate:** *"I see God in everything. I recognize and celebrate my union with everything because I am never alone. That which created me of the One Mind holds me and guides me always."*

> **When feeling resistance:** *"No less than the stars themselves shine a path of light as I travel*

on my spiritual journey. I let go and allow
God's love to give me courage, strength, and
clarity. I am filled with peace as I surrender."

Living on the other side of fear is not about being fearless. It is about understanding the rich and vital benefits of fear. Fear is a powerful motivator and creator. It is a guide that takes us on our journey. It is an emotion that brings us to our knees to pray and to demand answers.

Love is all these things and more. It is a powerful motivator and creator and a guide that takes us on our journey. It is an emotion that brings us to our knees as we pray and give thanks for the answers. Love is the emotion that we use to become spiritually conscious. It is the emotion that brings us to our essence.

This has been the story of my dance with fear and love. I have endured much pain, suffered emotionally and physically, and have caved in many times to self-defeating experiences. I have also reached heights of joy that I never imagined were possible. I have blossomed as a beautiful woman inside and out, and I feel magic in the richness of being in love with life. I share my story with you so that I can continue to heal and lift myself into the heaven of this earth. And I also share my story with you so that you may find strength within yourself, no matter what your story is. May this writing bless and comfort you as it has me. And may it bring you faith in the power and resiliency of the human spirit.

Little Bolts of Light

In the beginning there was Love.
And Love is all there is.

Affirmation:

I am never ending —
I am only beginning!

Affirmations

- ❤ I choose to live.
- ❤ I accept what I cannot understand.
- ❤ I like all of me, and I know I am always growing into who I think I am.
- ❤ What I give my thoughts to, that I create more of.
- ❤ I never give up; I expect a miracle.
- ❤ Gratitude sustains and heals me.
- ❤ The present moment is my greatest gift.
- ❤ The most important relationship I have is my relationship with God.
- ❤ My life has a spiritual purpose.
- ❤ I release my attachment to the outcome, and I trust in the highest and best for me now.
- ❤ God has already given me everything. I only need to become conscious of this.
- ❤ I always have enough time to do what I love.
- ❤ I honor my body as my spiritual vessel.
- ❤ I am in my perfect place for manifesting my blessings.
- ❤ I accept the foundation of my life as the perfect place to have come from.
- ❤ I am never ending–I am only beginning!

About the Author

$\mathcal{H}$ilda Villaverde is a teacher and minister with a passion for living. In her counseling and writing she facilitates self-discovery, empowerment, and transformation for those who are ready to embrace a spirit-filled life. She is a gifted speaker and workshop facilitator who shares her personal experiences with perspective and humor. Her workshops address important stages of life's journey: living beyond fear, taking risks, creating abundance, and developing spiritually.

Hilda incorporates her Yaqui Indian heritage and her love and respect for people to teach that we are "one in spirit, one in thought, and one in relationships."

Hilda is also a business woman and entrepreneur. She is the owner of a successful hairstyling salon in Scottsdale, Arizona, and the founder and president of the non-profit Vision Gatherings, Inc., a spiritual and professional networking organization.

If you would like information on workshops or speaking engagements in your area, or if you would like to schedule one, you may contact Hilda at: (800)584-1989, FAX 480-657-9355, or e-mail her at hildapluma@aol.com.